A Unifying Light

BOOKS OF ORIGINAL AND TRANSLATED VERSE BY MARTIN BIDNEY

Series: East-West Bridge Builders

Volume I: *East-West Poetry:*
A Western Poet Responds to Islamic Tradition in Sonnets, Hymns, and Songs
State University of New York Press

Volume II: J. W. von Goethe, *East-West Divan:*
The Poems, with "Notes and Essays": Goethe's Intercultural Dialogues
(translation from the German with original verse commentaries)
State University of New York Press

Volume III: *Poems of Wine and Tavern Romance:*
A Dialogue with the Persian Poet Hafiz
(translated from von Hammer's German versions, with original verse commentaries)
State University of New York Press

Volume IV: *A Unifying Light:*
Lyrical Responses to the Qur'an
Dialogic Poetry Press

Other Books

Alexander Pushkin, *Like a Fine Rug of Erivan: West-East Poems*
(trilingual with audio, co-translated from Russian and
co-edited with Bidney's Introduction)
Mommsen Foundation / Global Scholarly Publications

Saul Tchernikhovsky, *Lyrical Tales and Poems of Jewish Life*
(translated from the Russian versions of Vladislav Khodasevich)
Keshet Press

A Poetic Dialogue with Adam Mickiewicz: The "Crimean Sonnets"
(translated from the Polish, with Sonnet Preface, Sonnet Replies, and Notes)
Bernstein-Verlag Bonn

Enrico Corsi and Francesca Gambino, *Divine Adventure: The Fantastic Travels of Dante*
(English verse rendition of the prose translation by Maria Vera Properzi-Altschuler)
Idea Publications

[For e-books of verse and works of criticism see martinbidney.com]

A Unifying Light
LYRICAL RESPONSES TO THE QUR'AN

MARTIN BIDNEY

with six illustrations by Shahid Alam

VOLUME IV IN THE SERIES:
EAST-WEST BRIDGE BUILDERS

Dialogic
Poetry
Press

Copyright © 2015 by Martin Bidney
Vestal, New York

All Rights Reserved

ISBN 13: 978-1515369233
ISBN 10: 1515369234

Printed in the United States of America

Available from Amazon at http://www.amazon.com/dp/1515369234

This book is gratefully dedicated to

Ibrahim Abouleish,

Shahid Alam,

and

Katharina Mommsen

POEM OF TRIBUTE

to Ibrahim Abouleish, Shahid Alam, Katharina Mommsen

How fine: the name of Abraham or Ibrahim
Was given to the man who in our colloquies
Had brought three texts together in their harmonies
And lucidly revealed their Unifying Gleam.

And "witness of the world" another friend must be
Called rightly—Sháhid Álam, whose calligraphies
In paint and sculpture praise in shape and hue to please
The One Whose names are beauty, as we come to see.

And Katharina, you have guided me for years,
Progressing on the path of Goethe's bright Diván,
Sweet task for me—poetic joy to carry on:
To seek the Light that mind, heart, spirit-life endears.

The Unifying Light to link the West and East
Is heaven-beckoning to join an Eden feast.

CONTENTS

Illustrations: Works of Art by Shahid Alam   xiii
Introduction   xv
  (1) The Qur'an of Allah: "Lord of the Daybreak"   xvi
  (2) Three Texts, One Light: Serene Joy of Shared Wonder   xx
  (3) Centrality of Metaphor: "Let There be Light,"
     Let There Be Likeness   xxiv
  (4) Parable Narratives of Scriptural People:
     Illuminating Examples   xxix
  (5) Love as Unifying Moral Light:
     Radiant States of Being and Modes of Loving Action   xxxvi
     a) Generosity   xxxvii
     b) Peace of Mind   xxxix
     c) Forgiveness   xl
     d) Stewardship   xli
  (6) Influences from Islamic Tradition and Elsewhere   xliii

LYRICAL RESPONSES

1. To Sura 1 "The Opening," Verses in Sura 5 "The Table Spread"   1
2. To the Title of Sura 1 "The Opening"   2
3. To Verses in Sura 1 "The Opening"   3
4. To a Verse in Sura 2 "The Cow"   4
5. To Verses in Suras 2 "The Cow," 33 "The Clans"   5
6. To Verses in Sura 2 "The Cow"   6
7. To Verses in Sura 2 "The Cow"   7
8. To a Verse in Sura 2 "The Cow," 5 "The Table Spread"   9
9. To a Verse in Sura 2 "The Cow"   10
10. To a Verse in Sura 2 "The Cow"   11
11. To a Verse in Sura 2 "The Cow"   12
12. To a Verse in Sura 2 "The Cow"   13
13. To a Verse in Sura 2 "The Cow"   14
14. To Verses in Suras 2 "The Cow," 10 "Jonah"   15
15. To a Verse in Sura 2 "The Cow"   16
16. To Verses in Sura 2 "The Cow"   18

17. To Verses in Sura 2 "The Cow" — 20
18. To Verses in Sura 2 "The Cow" — 21
19. To a Verse in Sura 2 "The Cow," Talmud Verse — 22
20. To a Verse in Sura 2 "The Cow" — 23
21. To Verses in Suras 3 "The Family of 'Imrân," 24 "Light" — 24
22. To Verses in Suras 3 "The Family of 'Imrân," 62 "The Congregation" — 26
23. To Verses in Suras 3 "The Family of 'Imrân," 39 "The Troops" — 27
24. To Verses in Suras 4 "Women," 5 "The Table Spread," 6 "Cattle," 42 "Counsel" — 28
25. To Verses in Sura 5 "The Table Spread" — 29
26. To a Verse from Sura 5 "The Table Spread" — 30
27. To Verses in Sura 5 "The Table Spread" — 32
28. To a Verse in Sura 6 "Cattle" — 33
29. To a Verse in Sura 6 "Cattle" — 34
30. To a Verse in Sura 6 "Cattle" — 35
31. To a Verse in Sura 7 "The Heights" — 36
32. To Verses in Suras 7 "The Heights," 25 "The Criterion" — 37
33. To Verses in Suras 7 "The Heights," 59 "Exile," 73 "The Enshrouded One" — 38
34. To Verses in Suras 7 "The Heights," 12 "Joseph," 21 "The Prophets," 23 "The Believers" — 39
35. To Verses in Sura 7 "The Heights" — 40
36. To a Verse in Sura 9 "Repentance" — 41
37. To Verses in Sura 9 "Repentance" — 42
38. To Verses in Sura 10 "Jonah" — 43
39. To Verses in Suras 10 "Jonah," 14 "Abraham," 36 "Yâ Sîn" — 44
40. To Verses in Sura 10 "Jonah" — 45
41. To a Verse in Sura 10 "Jonah" — 46
42. To Verses in Suras 12 "Joseph," 53 "The Star" — 47
43. To Suras 12 "Joseph," 79 "'Those Who Drag Forth'" — 49
44. To Suras 12 "Joseph," 23 "The Believers" — 51
45. To Verses in Suras 12 "Joseph," 75 "The Raising of the Dead," 89 "The Dawn" — 53
46. To Verses in Sura 15 "Al-Ḥijr" — 55
47. To Verses in Sura 15 "Al-Ḥijr" — 57
48. To Verses in Sura 16 "The Bee" — 58
49. To Verses in Sura 16 "The Bee" — 59
50. To Verses in Sura 16 "The Bee" — 60
51. To Verses in Sura 16 "The Bee" — 61

52.	To Verses in Suras 16 "The Bee," 17 "The Children of Israel"	62
53.	To a Verse in Sura 17 "The Children of Israel"	63
54.	To Verses in Sura 17 "The Children of Israel"	64
55.	To Verses in Sura 17 "The Children of Israel"	65
56.	To Verses in Sura 17 "The Children of Israel," 30 "The Romans"	66
57.	To Verses in Sura 19 "Mary"	68
58.	To Verses in Sura 19 "Mary"	69
59.	To Verses in Sura 19 "Mary"	70
60.	To Verses in Sura 19 "Mary"	71
61.	To Verses in Suras 19 "Mary," 20 "Tâ Hâ"	72
62.	To Verses in Sura 20 "Tâ Hâ"	73
63.	To Verses in Suras 20 "Tâ Hâ," 75 "The Raising of the Dead"	74
64.	To Verses in Sura 21 "The Prophets"	75
65.	To Verses in Sura 21 "The Prophets"	76
66.	To a Verse in Sura 22 "The Pilgrimage"	77
67.	To Verses in Sura 23 "The Believers"	79
68.	To Verses in Suras 23 "The Believers," 25 "The Criterion"	80
69.	To Verses in Suras 23 "The Believers," 28 "The Story," 41 "Fuṣilat"	82
70.	To a Verse in Sura 24 "Light"	84
71.	To Verses in Suras 25 "The Criterion," 84 "The Sundering"	85
72.	To Verses in Sura 25 "The Criterion"	86
73.	To Verses in Sura 25 "The Criterion"	87
74.	To Verses in Sura 26 "The Poets"	89
75.	To Verses in Sura 26 "The Poets"	90
76.	To a Verse in Sura 27 "The Ant"	91
77.	To a Verse in Sura 27 "The Ant"	92
78.	To Verses in Sura 28 "The Story"	93
79.	To Verses in Suras 28 "The Story," 66 "Banning"	95
80.	To Verses in Sura 30 "The Romans"	96
81.	To a Verse in Sura 30 "The Romans"	97
82.	To Verses in Sura 31 "Luqmân"	99
83.	To a Verse in Sura 31 "Luqmân"	100
84.	To Verses in Sura 32 "The Prostration"	101
85.	To Verses in Sura 33 "The Clans"	102
86.	To a Verse in Sura 33 "The Clans"	103
87.	To Verses in Suras 33 "The Clans," 34 "Saba"	104
88.	To Verses in Sura 33 "The Clans"	105
89.	To a Verse in Sura 33 "The Clans"	107
90.	To Verses in Sura 34 "Saba"	108
91.	To Verses in Sura 34 "Saba"	110

92. To Verses in Sura 35 "The Angels"	111
93. To Verses in Sura 37, "Those Who Set the Ranks"	112
94. To Verses in Sura 37 "Those Who Set the Ranks"	114
95. To Verses in Sura 37 "Those Who Set the Ranks"	115
96. To Verses in Sura 38 "Ṣad"	116
97. To Verses in Sura 38 "Ṣad"	117
98. To Verses in Sura 39 "The Troops"	118
99. To Verses in Sura 39 "The Troops"	119
100. To Verses in Sura 39 "The Troops"	120
101. To Verses in Sura 40 "The Believer"	121
102. To Verses in Sura 41 "Fuṣilat"	122
103. To Verses in Sura 42 "Counsel"	123
104. To a Verse in Sura 42 "Counsel"	124
105. To a Verse in Sura 42 "Counsel"	125
106. To a Verse in Sura 47 "Muhammad"	126
107. To a Verse in Sura 24 "Light"	127
108. To a Verse in Sura 48 "Victory"	128
109. To Verses in Sura 49 "The Private Apartments"	129
110. To Verses in Sura 50 "Qâf"	130
111. To Verses in Sura 50 "Qâf"	132
112. To a Verse in Sura 53 "The Star"	133
113. To Verses in Sura 53 "The Star"	134
114. To Verses in Sura 53 "The Star"	135
115. To Verses in Sura 55 "The Beneficent"	136
116. To Verses in Suras 55 "The Beneficent," 56 "The Event"	137
117. To Verses in Suras 56 "The Event," 57 "Iron"	138
118. To a Verse in Sura 59 "Exile"	139
119. To a Verse in Sura 59 "Exile"	140
120. To a Verse in Sura 63 "The Hypocrites"	141
121. To Verses in Sura 64 "Mutual Disillusion"	142
122. To Verses in Sura 64 "Mutual Disillusion"	143
123. To a Verse in Sura 67 "The Sovereignty"	145
124. To Verses in Sura 70 "The Ascending Stairways"	146
125. To Verses in Sura 70 "The Ascending Stairways"	147
126. To Verses in Sura 72 "The Jinn"	148
127. To Verses in Sura 73 "The Enshrouded One"	149
128. To Verses in Sura 76 "'Time' or 'Man'"	150
129. To Verses in Sura 78 "The Tidings"	152
130. To Verses in Sura 80 "'He Frowned'"	153
131. To Verses in Sura 80 "'He Frowned'"	154

132.	To Verses in Sura 84 "The Sundering"	155
133.	To Verses in Sura 85 "The Mansions of the Stars"	156
134.	To Verses in Sura 86 "The Morning Star"	157
135.	To Verses in Suras 86 "The Morning Star," 96 "The Clot"	159
136.	To Verses in Sura 91 "The Sun"	160
137.	To Sura 93 "The Morning Hours"	161
138.	To Sura 94 "Solace"	162
139.	To Sura 94 "Solace"	163
140.	To Sura 97 "Power"	166

Concluding Thought: The Naming of Angels	169
Selected Annotated Bibliography	171
Index	175

ILLUSTRATIONS
Works of Art by Shahid Alam

Front cover: "ILM," sculpture presenting the Arabic word for "Knowledge" or "Wisdom." The form of the work combines the three Arabic letters *'ayin, lam, mim,* or *i, l,* and *m* in such a way that the word is instantly readable by anyone who knows written Arabic.

Plate I: "Nurullah, Ruhullah, Habibullah" ("Light of God, Spirit of God, Love of God"). These are traditionally held to be, respectively, the three distinctive contributions of Moses, Jesus, and Muhammad, the three teachers of the one Abrahamic religion that is variously embodied in Judaism, Christianity, and Islam.

Plate II: "Musa, Issa, Muhammad" ("Moses, Jesus, Muhammad"). These are the three teachers of the Abrahamic religion of the One God. Note that the triangles here are equilateral. The equal sides are of equal importance to the triangular structure.

Plate III: "IQRA" ("Recite!"). This was the command given by Archangel Gabriel to the Prophet Muhammad on the Night of Power (note the prominence of the nocturnal colors blue and black in the picture), when Muhammad was enabled by the strength of Allah to recite the Qur'an. Like the front cover sculpture, this painting presents the letters of an Arabic word. Here it is the word which means "read" or "recite."

Plate IV: "Allah-Menorah." The name of Allah or God is written in Arabic twice in mirror fashion, and the two occurrences of the final letter H are done in green, the holy color of the Prophet Muhammad. This letter symbolizes breathing or breath, lifegiving creative power. The seven vertically pointing forms recall the seven branches of the Sabbath candle-holder in Judaism, and the joining of the central stem of the candelabra to the branches recalls the cross, emblem of Christianity.

Back cover: "ALIF," sculpture representing the first letter of the Arabic alphabet, suggesting also the first appearance of the Light of the Creation of the world by God in the Judeo-Christo-Islamic tradition.

INTRODUCTION

The book you are holding is a poet's response to reading a venerable and vivid work of scripture, the Qur'an. Though not a Muslim by upbringing, as I put together this collection of lyric verse for Muslim and non-Muslim alike, I again felt granted imaginative insight by an extended encounter with this founding text of Islam. I don't read Arabic, but in the 1930 English rendering by Mohammed Marmaduke Pickthall I found, and continue to discover, an engaging depth and a vigorous, nuanced beauty. The Prophet Muhammad said that God Himself wrote the Qur'an, and that he, a messenger, only spoke it forth. There is so much to treasure in Pickthall's rendering of what has been called God's own poetry (Alam, *Gottespoesie*) that I felt drawn to reply with the best word-melodies I could make. The chanting or hearing of the Qur'an in Arabic is meant to be a musical experience. Listening to it on internet, I like to draw parallels to Hebrew biblical cantillation and Gregorian ecclesiastical chant. Though it is generally said to be in prose, the Qur'an features emphatic rhythm patterns, rhymes, and resonant poetic metaphors. Islam teaches that God loves beauty and creates beauty: "His are the most beautiful names" (Qur'an 20:8, poem 61); indeed, the ninety-nine offered in the Qur'an are recited as a meditation, counted with beads on what one might call an Islamic rosary (poems 119, 128). The Lord made His Qur'an pleasant to speak, "easy in thy tongue" (19:97), a joy to hear.

Rather than a theological commentary, you will find here a set of lyrical replies to Qur'anic passages. The reply-poems are the responses of a grateful ponderer, a crafted journal of the feelings engendered by Qur'anic portions that attracted me. My custom, for some months, had been to open the text almost daily, sampling any page I encountered (see poem 66) for poetic stimulus. In the same way, the book I've written is suited to random browsing. It follows the order of suras or chapters in the Qur'an, but those chapters are arranged by decreasing length (the brief initial orienting sura excepted), and there is no conventional unifying narrative structure. The Qur'an is eminently worth reading for those of any religion, or of none. But, in addition, a reader familiar with either the Hebrew Bible or the Christian Gospels will likely feel at home and at ease in the Islamic Qur'an, for it foregrounds themes and narratives from both traditions. It offers a unifying light.

The Qur'an has a structure not linear but circular and radial. The conceptual center is the one God, with His creative attributes and their implications for human conduct. The primal creative power of God's word is symbolized by the *alif*, first letter of the Arabic alphabet, the single straight line that incised light into the darkness (see the illustrative sculpture by Shahid Alam on the back cover; also poem 1). From this primal Unifying Light at the center radiate references to Allah's myriad works and ways, and allusions to Jewish and Christian scriptural narratives similarly extend outward in many directions. The illumination from the Sun of the Qur'an, its light-giving "Lord of the Daybreak" (113:1), includes the illuminings offered by the three other holy books of Islam: Torah, Gospels (each of these two volumes being called a "guidance and a light"—5:44, 46, poem 1), and Psalms. Circular, non-linear structure has led some to formulate a surprising intercultural aesthetic:

> Many authors have pointed to the similarities between the writing style of the Koran and the works of James Joyce. For example, Umberto Eco once said that we will only be able to understand the Koran once we have learnt to understand Joyce. Such opinions are related to Joyce's attempt to write a story [*Finnegans Wake*] which was neither 'historical' nor causal. Literary critics talk of a metahistorical level, anachronisms and a history *sub specie aeternitatis*: 'with an eye on eternity'. . . . It is indeed indisputable that there is a remarkable affinity between the most openly 'defiant' of all sacred texts and the most avant-garde literary experiment of all time. Joyce was perfectly aware of this affinity. Of the 114 suras of the Koran, no fewer than 111 are referred to in *Finnegans Wake*. (Colpaert 101–102)

(1) The Qur'an of Allah: "Lord of the Daybreak"

Islam, the religion of surrender to Allah, or God, the "Lord of the Daybreak" (113:1), holds four texts from three traditions to be divinely revealed in its unifying light. These are (1) the Five Books of Moses, also called the Torah, Pentateuch, or Law [*Tawrāt*]; (2) the Psalms of David [*Zabur*]; (3) the Gospels of Matthew, Mark, Luke, and John [*Injil*, related to "evangel," which is Greek for "good tidings"]; and (4) the Qur'an. People from the Jewish and Christian holy books reappear extensively in that of Islam, where we learn a great deal more about them. These facts about Islam had startled me as much as they had surprised Kathy, the wife-to-be of Abdulrahman Zeitoun, a Syrian-American hero who attempted to rescue people in New Orleans after Hurricane Katrina in Dave Eggers' nonfiction novel *Zeitoun*.

Kathy had no idea, for instance, that the Qur'an was filled with the same people as the Bible—"Moses, Mary, Abraham, Pharaoh, even Jesus. She hadn't known that Muslims consider the Qur'an the fourth book of God to His messengers . . ." (Eggers 61). Indeed, "Mary appears more times in the Quran than in the New Testament," and "Muslims also believe in the virgin birth of Jesus" (Esposito 2011, 78). The Torah is "mentioned in the Quran eighteen times as true revelation that preceded the Gospels and the Quran" (Esposito, ed. 2003, 321). "God is considered the author of the psalms. Sura 21:105 is a direct counterpart of the biblical Psalm 37:29" (Esposito, ed. 250). Even a seemingly minor prophet is highly regarded: "Yunus [Jonah] is so central to Islam that an entire chapter in the Koran bears his name, an honor bestowed on only five other biblical figures: Abraham, Noah, Joseph, Mary, and the Queen of Sheba" (Feiler 2007, 255).

Ethical teachings of the two earlier-taught religions derived from Abraham are also elaborated and united in the third, and in its scripture, the Qur'an. Pakistani-born German artist Shahid Alam has made a colored calligraphic painting (Plate I) to show the distinctive contributions of the three teachers of Islam as traditionally summarized. These are (1) *nurúllah*, or the Light of God, introduced by Moses; (2) *ruhúllah* or the Spirit of God, invoked by Jesus; and (3) *habíbullah* or the Love of God, emphasized by Muhammad. One widely used Islamic teaching tool is an equilateral triangle with the Arabic words *Musa* [Moses], *Issa* [Jesus], *Muhammad* written along the *three mutually supporting sides of equal length*. Shahid has made a calligraphy of this, too, that I cherish (Plate II). The symbolic import is widening and unifying: *Light, Spirit, and Love are one.* They include, enclose, enfold the One.

Between 20 and 25 percent of the world's people are Muslims. There are 41 Muslim-majority countries. It is predicted that by the year 2070 Islam will likely have more adherents than any other religion. The Qur'an is a series of revelations that the Prophet Muhammad received beginning in 610 CE when he was 40 years old. For 1500 years now, Islam has been developing a legacy of belief, action, and poetic expression based on one decisive event, the granting of the Qur'an by Allah, Arabic for "the God" or "the Lord." This major uniting event in the religious, cultural, and literary history of the world resulted from a terrifying encounter, which proved beneficial only when the seeming peril had been surmounted. According to tradition, when Angel Gabriel told Muhammad to read the Qur'an, the latter could neither read nor write: "He it is Who hath sent among the unlettered ones a messenger of their own, to recite unto them His revelations and to make them grow, and to teach them the Scripture and Wisdom" (62:2). Muhammad was at first not only baffled but alarmed, wondering if

Plate I

he were possessed by a jinn, a pernicious fiery spirit (poem 137). The *hadith* or memoir literature makes clear the shock of the encounter—and also Muhammad's tormented hesitation, until he yielded and was miraculously empowered to read.

Rainer Maria Rilke re-envisioned the astounding moment in a poem, "Muhammad's Calling" ("Mohammeds Berufung"), which I'll translate:

> Into his hiding place upon the height
> What we know well had swiftly happened. He,
> The angel, came—tall, pure, in blazing light.
> All protest waved aside, he pressingly
>
> Asked—tired, bewildered merchant (that is all
> He was), of travel weary, a delay:
> He'd never read before, and now to say
> Such words—a *wise* man would the task appall.
>
> The angel, though, commanded, showed—indeed
> *Again* showed what upon that page was writ—
> Would not give up but urged, insisted: *Read*.

A UNIFYING LIGHT

xix

> And so he read—so that the angel bowed—
> And was now one who had *recited* it,
> Was able, heard, had done it, was allowed.

The bafflement, resistance, and final yielding are mirrored in the poem's halting rhythm and struggling syntax, both in Rilke's German and in my English rendering.

But the yielding was a triumph for the illumined one—who appeared "tall, pure, in blazing light," as Rilke says. Later, Muhammad would even have the satisfaction of hearing from the very lips of the Lord that a "com-

Plate II

pany of the Jinn" [fiery spirits] had thought the Qur'an "marvellous" and had converted to Islam (72:1–2, poem 126). Alone among the three scriptures in the Judeo-Christo-Islamic tradition, the Qur'an is the recital, by one person, of the revelation he receives. Rilke mentions a "page," but in fact the Qur'an refers to no pages, no parchment, metal, marble, no material text—a fact leading mystical Sufi interpreters to suggest that Muhammad was reading directly from the divine heart of the universe (poem 116). The command the Prophet received—"Iqra!"—means not only "Read!" but "Recite!" Angel Gabriel's command was a call to proclaim good tidings, to make them heard. In Shahid Alam's calligraphic painting the word "Iqra" (Plate III) is lent an atmosphere that conveys not only the urgency and beauty of the message, but even an awed feeling of the angelic presence.

(2) Three Texts, One Light: Serene Joy of Shared Wonder

Abraham is the first proponent of monotheism according to Jewish, Christian, and Islamic scripture, and his revered emblematic stature unites the three. The central orienting statements of the three Abrahamic religions are each embodied in a stirring text combining simplicity with grandeur. These are Judaism's "Hear O Israel," Christianity's "Our Father," and Islam's "The Opening," initial sura of the Qur'an. Let me place them side by side. When read in sequence, they prove kindred expressions of a single mood:

> Deut. 6:4. Hear O Israel: The Lord our God is one Lord;
> 5. And thou shalt love the Lord thy God with all thine heart, and with all thy soul, and with all thy might.
> 6. And these words, which I command thee this day, shall be in thine heart:
> 7. And thou shalt teach them diligently unto thy children, and shalt talk of them when thou sittest in thine house, and when thou walkest by the way, and when thou liest down, and when thou risest up.
> 8. And thou shalt bind them for a sign upon thine hand, and they shall be as frontlets between thine eyes.
> 9. And thou shalt write them upon the posts of thine house, and on thy gates.

~~~~~

Plate III

Matt. 6:9. Our Father which art in heaven, Hallowed be thy name.
10. Thy kingdom come, Thy will be done in earth, as it is in heaven.
11. Give us this day our daily bread.
12. And forgive us our debts, as we forgive our debtors.
13. And lead us not into temptation, but deliver us from evil; For thine is the kingdom, and the power, and the glory, for ever. Amen.

~~~~~

Sûrah 1 The Opening.
In the name of Allah, the Beneficent, the Merciful.
1. Praise be to Allah, Lord of the Worlds,
2. The Beneficent, the Merciful.
3. Owner of the Day of Judgment,
4. Thee (alone) we worship; Thee (alone) we ask for help.
5. Show us the straight path,
6. The path of those whom Thou hast favoured;
7. Not (the path) of those who earn Thine anger nor of those who go astray.

Each focusing on the one God, the paragraphs reveal a clear kinship of thought and feeling.

What I offer is a journal of lyrical replies to Qur'anic passages that deeply stirred me. And one reason I present these three convergent statements at the beginning of the journal is that, like the Qur'an itself, they together convey a heartening poetic depth of spirit. More specifically for my purpose, they mirror, because they helped establish, the mindset I am working from: *a serene joy of shared wonder*. One may express the theme equally well as combining *the centrality of the heart* with *awed awareness of the unbounded*. I don't find much intercultural scripture-reading going on today. But when a Jew reads the Gospels and the Qur'an, when a Muslim reads the Jewish and Christian sacred writings, or when a Christian reads both the Hebraic Bible and the holy book of Islam, all the readers may alike begin to see how united, indeed how mutually illuminating, the three traditions are in their poetic power, moral message, love and awe. The three orienting texts you have just read underline the shared awareness.

I have gathered an array of unifying material interrelating the kindred Abrahamic legacies by way of Qur'anic epigraphs or introductory quotations. I subjoin to these my own poetic responses that may also embody perspectives of the other two traditions—as well as additional viewpoints (more on this below). It is a dialogic endeavor, a pioneering technique meant to broaden imagination, to build bridges. I intend this collection as a bringing together, for as the Qur'an avers, "Wheresoever ye may be, Allah will bring you all together" (2:148, poem 12). It is an invitation to advance world peace. In our current era of often irrational conflict, an attempt at mutual understanding is timely. We can try to dispel needless conflict by receptive comprehension.

We don't live in a poetical age, prose being far more popular. But, to the imaginative mind, the charm and stimulation of the three convergent orienting texts quoted above are centrally bound up with their rhythms and cadences, their melodic patternings of sound. For me, the only adequate literary response to them must be lyrical. It is lyrics, word music, that they, and—even more—the Qur'an passages that captivate the poetic impulse, are asking me to write. And music is an irresistible unifying power. As the gifted nineteenth-century scholar-poet and Qur'an translator Friedrich Rückert put it, "Weltpoesie allein ist Weltversöhnung," "world poetry alone is world conciliation" (Rückert 1833, 6). The directive to "let it be"—giving life to all existent things—harmonized and united them in the shared light of a creative act.

To a reader who wants to reply to poetry with more poetry, the serene joy of shared wonder that my three orienting texts convey can be felt as the poetic-emotional mood and atmosphere of them all, their unifying mutual attunement or shared illumination. It isn't at all hard to understand how the miracle of life in a fathomless pluriverse can be loved with all one's "heart," "soul," and "might" (Jewish wording) as a hallowed sovereignty of "power" and "glory" (Christian wording). The myriad of worlds, and the unexplainable wonder of a human awareness that can celebrate them and their unwordable source (poem 22, 5–8), can together convey to the poet a feeling as of being impelled and protected by a guardianship "beneficent" and "merciful" (Islamic wording). Such a feeling of awe and mystery, arousing gratitude (poem 76) and a "solemn joy" (poem 33), is the origin of my poems here. I sensed it as the informing mentality of the Qur'an, whose radial structure with God at the radiant center one might try to emulate, formally, in a non-linear book with shared wonder at the core.

The same feeling stimulated authors in the modern era whose Islam-related lyric writings I had, in recent years, the privilege to translate. These writers include the greatest poets of three countries, who are acknowledged as such by virtually all students of the respective national literatures. The writers are Russia's greatest poet Alexander Pushkin ("Imitations of the Qur'an," "The Prophet"), Poland's greatest poet Adam Mickiewicz ("Crimean Sonnets"), and—most important for my own development—the two bards' mentor and Germany's greatest poet, Johann Wolfgang von Goethe (*West-East Divan*). All three of these creators—each a word artist of world caliber—are pathbreakers, builders of bridges.

The inclusive theme of the joy of shared wonder brings me back to a point made earlier: two of the four divinely revealed books of Islam are Jewish and one is Christian. The uniting of the three traditions in Qur'anic thought and feeling comes through in many poems where I reply to passages on the relation of the Torah and Gospels to the Qur'an. The scripture verses 5:44–48 on the mutually reinforcing, unifying light of Torah, Gospels, and Qur'an help me interpret Sura 1 "The Opening" (poems 1, 25). The theme of unification unfolds as the book proceeds (5:68–69, poem 8; 5:110, poems 26, 27; 7:156–157, poem 35). A reference to the many visionaries favored by Allah moved me to mention important prophets named in the Qur'an (3:84, poem 23). Replying to 17:55 (poem 53) I offer, as poet, grateful thoughts about the heartening inclusion of the lyrical musician David in the list. When Allah compares the righteous to the sown corn, He notes that His metaphor is found in the Jewish and Christian scriptures (48:29, poem 108). Imaginatively, geographically, the insight unifies: "Unto Allah belong the East and the West" (2:142, poem 11).

(3) Centrality of Metaphor: "Let There Be Light," Let There Be Likeness

This uniting theme of likeness or symbolic metaphor, along with a related theme, the parable or exemplary narrative, is treated often in the Qur'an. The Hellenic-derived word *meta-phor* means a bearing-beyond, while *sym-bol* means a throwing-together (poems 56, 107). Transcendences converge. Islamic statements on this topic may encourage the poet whose daily life is metaphor-making. Not only has Allah "coined for mankind in this Qur'ân all kinds of similitudes" (30:58, 39:27, poems 71, 80, 98), but He also treats, helpfully and often, the question of allegorical versus literal interpretation. The role of metaphor as a means of understanding Allah with the heart, mind, and spirit is crucial because the languages of mortals are finite and fallible, while Plenitude of Being is unutterable and inconceivable.

The leap from zero to one—from nothing to a thing—is only a single digit in arithmetic, but it feels like an infinity when qualitatively, ontologically considered. The schoolchild learns that 0 + 1 = 1. But the poet, overwhelmed by the infinite distance in reality-value between something and nothing at all, may prefer to write 0 + Infinity = 1. Since our human speech cannot grasp with concepts the heart-stopping leap from zero to Being, from nothingness to worlds unnumbered, we have to use figurative, exploratory language. Likeness, emblem, and parable might guide us, in part, on the unmappable ocean. We cannot avoid using *metaphor*. But we can use it to the limit of our capacity for depth of feeling, breadth of comprehension, and height of aspiring.

The unifying potentials of metaphor, symbol, sign, portent, and parable are explored with care (2:164, poem 13; 16:69, poems 50, 51; 17:89, poem 56; 41:39, poem 102; 39:17, poem 56). In the last of these Qur'anic readings we find particular interest, for here we learn that "His [Allah's] is the one Sublime Similitude in the heavens and in the earth" (poems 56, 81). In poem 140 I suggest, "The Lord by metaphor alone / Can spoken be with poet-might." That is because, in responding to Sura 97, "The Night of Power," it occurred to me that the humbling and triumphant night when Muhammad, with Angel Gabriel's aid, was first granted Qur'anic wisdom may point to precisely the Sublime Similitude which is that of God Himself—the unifying light of height-and-depth that is at the same time dark to finite beings. As the mystic philosopher who traditionally goes by the name of Dionysius the Areopagite (late fifth to early sixth century CE) has argued, all talk about God is metaphor.

No mortal, finite words can be adequate to name or describe directly what Dionysius named the Superluminous Darkness. One may feel the awe that overcame this humble and judicious thinker when one contemplates the metaphoric implications of the Night of Power in the Qur'an. The feeling-thought that concludes my series of scripture replies (poem 140) is the Power of that Night which is the Superluminous Dark. Central to this thought is the intimate kinship of unwordable bright-in-dark to the prophetic dream or trance that the poet treasures. Poets live by metaphor; and a thinker in likenesses, an ontologic imaginer, might seek by this means to envision the Sun-beyond-Sun, the asymptotic hidden illumination that language is reaching toward.

To God, then, belongs the one "Sublime Similitude." Qur'anic verses important for the uniting, harmonizing imagination are the following two statements about Allah's use of metaphor. (1) "Verily We have coined for mankind in this Qur'ān all kinds of similitudes" (30:58, poem 80). (2) ". . . His [God's] is the Sublime Similitude in the heavens and in the earth" (30:27, poems 80, 81). Not only the Qur'an but all the myriad created worlds are filled with similitudes—each a symbol, a likeness, a metaphor that God has coined. The "face" of the Lord—the word "Lord" itself—is such a metaphor (55:26–27, poem 115). "Creation" and "birth" of worlds are metaphors; any pronominal gender used in referring to the Ultimate is a metaphor. To Allah, the Ineffable or Unwordable, belongs the highest and most inclusive, the most widely embracing and deeply uniting of all metaphors (poem 110). It is the all-including "Sublime Similitude" of the Ultimate, emblemed as Unifying Light, that the Qur'an sets forth to be a poet's goal as a maker of likenesses and parables. From the Qur'anic standpoint, the challenge will gladden the heart, since the welcome task of reaching toward that Similitude is implied in the "good tidings" which the Prophet brought (33:45, poem 85). The task of metaphoric travel to that Similitude may be called an imaginative pilgrimage of the poet-mind away from limiting self-absorption toward vision-broadening source-metaphor (33:63, poem 86; 22:27, poem 66). Metaphors for this are all we have, and it is best that we share them.

A word should be inserted here about the metaphoric values inherent in outstanding examples of Islamic visual art. The qualities of beauty, formative originality, and meditation-friendly graceful shape in Shahid Alam's non-representational sculpture reproduced on the front cover of this book are intended as visual metaphors, likenesses of the Unutterable, the Truth of essential Being that they point toward. "Wisdom" or "Knowledge" is the meaning of the word ILM, whose three letters, welded together, constitute the sculpture, which can thus be "read" in more ways than one. Metaphoric wisdom can be embodied not only in the audible arts of lyric poetry and music, but in the visible ones of painting, sculpture, dance, and architecture. The symbolic rooms of the Taj Mahal are correlated to portions of the Qur'an.

Speaking in metaphor, allegory, or parable is a crucial tool in Qur'anic teaching. For that reason the Qur'an treats it profoundly, in a nuanced, balanced way. Like Plato, Muhammad is concerned that the message he brings not be mistaken for the imaginings of already-familiar poets. Nor should metaphoric speech be used for proud polemic, ill-humored quibbling: "those in whose hearts is doubt pursue . . . that which is allegorical[,] seeking (to cause) dissension by seeking to explain it" (3:7, poem 21). As a way to solve this problem, the allegory in the sura "Light" (24:35, poems 21, 70) communicates the import of a divine "similitude" so well that, putting argument aside, it lets you feel how light mediates between greater and lesser realms of Being, without dispelling the mystery of their linked existence.

Allah loves the light; metaphorically we may say He *is* the Unifying

Light. He is the "Lord of the Daybreak" (113:1)—and the rising Morning Star, herald of dawn, seems linked at once to the ideas of a spirit-guardian and of the "gushing fluid" from which we came (6:97, 86:1–7, poems 134, 135). The sun and its light are like the soul and its growth (91:1–10, poem 136). The core and height of cosmic and moral meaning in Qur'anic metaphors will distinguish them from shallow poetic likenesses. Further, any given metaphor may be a spiritual preparation for a yet higher one. When God gave Moses the commandments, He sent the mountain "crashing down" (7:143). But when He gave Muhammad the Qur'an, He judged that we no longer needed a cataclysmic likeness of the humbling of the high by the Awe of the Almighty (59:21; poem 33), being now worthy of the subtler but higher metaphor of Light. There is a mystical quality to this unifying Light, combining the immanent and the transcendent, the mind's knowledge and the heart's wonder (poem 21).

The unifying light proposed by the Qur'an is embodied in Plate IV, the painting "Allah-Menorah" by Shahid Alam. The artist explains (and I translate the German): "The word 'Allah' at the center is written twice, in mirror-fashion. Seven vertical forms recall the seven candles of the menorah, the Jewish Sabbath candelabra. Together with the central stem, the branches form the Christian symbol of the cross. In the middle, in the representation of a green flame, is the double letter HA, concluding the twice-written name of Allah. This letter symbolizes breathing, or breath." The unity of Judaism, Christianity, and Islam presented in the Qur'an may be felt as the breath of a divine-and-human spiritual life, source and expression of a unifying light.

The practiced thinker in metaphor will understand that symbols need not be literalized: the seeker of illumination should not expect the Prophet to arrive in a company of angels, build a house of gold, make rivers gush forth, hand out dates and grapes (31:89–93, poems 54, 55). Rather, with such gifts we are endowed metaphorically, in the receptive and enlivened heart. Allah didn't want us "one community" with one culture and one language (10:20, poem 38). Rather, He created fruits, hills, people, beasts, cattle, all of "diverse hues" (35:27–28, poem 92).

For this reason, in the Qur'anic view the fall of the Tower of Babel is no tragedy, but an opportunity, an opening. It is not finally divisive but a spur to intercultural, interhuman understanding. Diversity lets us come to know one another (49:13), to know God through each other. Differing colors and cultures are a metaphoric spectrum of His unifying Light, even as the bee creates honey "diverse of hues" (16:69, poems 50, 51). For an invigorating illustration of the flexibility Allah shows, and teaches, in coining simili-

Plate IV

tudes we can look at 2:74 (poem 9). Here we learn that though a rock may suggest hard-heartedness, there are numberless other ways to think of rocks. Rivers may descend from rocky heights, a stone may be burst by a surging fountain, boulders may fall down as if in fear of God. To be true to nature's own ingenuity, our use of metaphor would need to be no less inventive.

For an area where allegory flourishes in the Qur'an, we may look to Heaven or to its analogy in Eden, the emblematic earthly paradise. Regarding "those who believe and do good works" we learn that "there are

Gardens underneath which rivers flow," and "as often as they [the Eden-dwellers] are regaled with the fruit thereof, they say: This is what was given us aforetime; and it is given to them in resemblance" (4:25, poem 4). Underground rivers allegorize unconscious dream-world powers alerting the poet to the source of our surprised awakening (poem 55). They emblemize motion, flow, lifegiving openness to change (poem 11; 2:164, poems 13, 22, 49, 108, 128). Earthly joys and paradisal ones may allegorize each other, for "... He it is Who maketh night a covering for you, and sleep repose, and maketh day a resurrection" (25:47, poem 73).

If each new day of our life is a resurrection, one sees how heavenly are many of the earthly wonders it would be lazy to take for granted, such as getting up in the morning, when the human creature is brought back to life by the literal and metaphoric Sun. Earth viewed wakefully—in Qur'anic terms—is already a heaven, a terrestrial paradise. Using earthly metaphor, we can easily picture the emblematic "maidens for companions" (78:33, poem 129) in Eden or Heaven, female spirits called houris, very like ministering angels, who serve an emblematic blessed wine of perfect purity, wine of the sort that flows in rivers of paradise (47:15). Of the "Gardens of Eden, which the Beneficent hath promised" to those rewarded "in the Unseen," we are further told: "They hear therein no idle talk, but only Peace; and therein they have food for morn and evening" (19:61–62, poem 60). Qur'an translator A. Yusuf Ali's note on the Arabic word for "Peace" allows me to suggest that the nourishing food and drink of Eden can itself be called a metaphor of the ideal of "Salām," combining "peace" and "surrender" or *Islam*. Allah "hath expanded" the human heart "for the Surrender" (39:22, poems 23, 98, 118).

In the condition of surrender Muhammad, according to one Sufi teaching, had read the Holy Scripture not by deciphering a material text but by peering into the deepest heart of the world (poem 116). Here, even the words "read" and "scripture" attain the level of mystical metaphors, leading us to the ontologic asymptote—unutterable awareness of the One "Sublime Similitude" (30:27). "Let there be light" means "Let there be likeness." Metaphor is a unifying light.

(4) Parable Narratives of Scriptural People: Illuminating Examples

Much of the Qur'an consists of narratives. There is a feast of these, and were it not that the Prophet tells us he did not write them but only received them from God, I would want to call Muhammad a literary genius. A Jew encountering for the first time what in Judaic tradition would appear as abundant Qur'anic *midrashím* or enriching interpretations of Abraham, Joseph, Moses, David, and Solomon might well be tempted to exclaim, "If Muhammad tells us these things, what a fine Jew he is!" A Christian coming first into contact with what in Christian tradition would appear as extra-biblical but loving and reverent parables of Mary, Jesus, and John the Baptist might similarly be tempted to respond, "If Muhammad can convey to us these ennobling narratives, what a fine Christian he is!" The Christian might be further impressed that Muhammad calls Jesus the Messiah (3:45, poem 58) and views Mary as the holy virgin whose child was born, with no human father, by the aid of the Spirit of God (21:91, poem 64). True, the three traditions have theological components which differ, but much that is universally valuable in the Jewish and Christian Bible stories will be refreshed, renewed, and deepened by a reading of the Qur'an. My poetical criterion of value is the veracity of feeling, of metaphors that issue from what John Keats called "the holiness of the heart's affections," what the Qur'an calls "beneficent" and "merciful" love.

In a scriptural tale, an episode in a person's life can become an illuminating parable of moral values, an exemplary or cautionary symbol. The tale of Adam and Eve is the plainest example: a story of a fall through the temptation of forbidden food, yet told, in the Qur'an, with emphasis on the quick relenting of God, "For lo! He is the Relenting, the Merciful" (2:35–39; poems 6, 7). Likewise the unprecedented action of Abraham, esteemed as originator of monotheism, in leaving his father's home to worship a new deity, can be called a parable in this sense. Because the Qur'an views biblical people in perspectives that may differ from either the Jewish or Christian ones, new parables abound.

Enjoyably, too, the novelty may combine with familiar elements. In the Qur'an, Abraham smashes his father's idols, all but the biggest of them, and when asked what happened replies, in effect, "The big one did it." When Abraham further offends the people and is put into a furnace to be burned alive (37:83–97; poems 93, 139), God makes the fire "coolness and peace" for him (21:69–69; poem 65). This tale of offense, punishment, and rescue cannot be located in Jewish scriptures, but it appears in the Judaic *Midrash Bereshith* 38:13. It is an effective parable of God's mercy (poem 65), thematically central to the Qur'an, where every sura or chapter begins with the words, "In the name of Allah, the Beneficent, the Merciful."

A winsome parable distinctive to the Qur'an is the episode where Abraham asks Allah to show him how the dead are resurrected. Allah tells him to place on four hills four birds that he has tamed, then watch them fly back to their master (2:260; poem 16)—a sacred fable of parental care and love, and of the grateful offspring's eventual return. Abraham's reception of the three biblical messengers is retold in the Qur'an, and here, too, emphasis on God's kindness and compassion is added. When Abraham shows initial fear of the strangers, they say, "We bring thee good tidings in truth. So be not thou of the despairing." Abraham then beautifully replies, "And who despaireth of the mercy of his Lord save those who are astray?" (15:55–56; poem 46). From the poet's point of view, perhaps the greatest favor the Qur'an does for Abraham is to attribute to him a profound, noble, melodious prayer, appropriately requesting Allah's merciful pardon for Abraham's erring father (26:83–39; poems 74, 75). So much of what is most heartening in the Qur'an may be found in this brief utterance of Abraham's that we are not surprised when Allah reminds His people that they should "be not divided" in teaching the one religion that inspired and united prophets from Noah to Muhammad, the same religion He "commended unto Abraham and Moses and Jesus" (42:13; poem 103).

Another word about Abraham's unifying status of Enlightener may be helpful. Throughout his book *Abraham: A Journey to the Heart of the Three Faiths* Bruce Feiler notes the range of attitudes in the three acknowledged Abrahamic traditions toward their prototypic founding pioneer. The uses made of Abraham have been at times dialogic and constructive, at other times rivalrously disuniting. In *Where God Was Born* Feiler observes:

> ... I discovered that while the biblical story of Abraham has a message of unity, each of the religions that grew from his line had reinterpreted the story for its own exclusive purposes. Abraham became as much a source of war as he was a seed of peace. (52–53)

But in *Juden Christen Muslime: Herkunft und Zukunft* ("Jews Christians Muslims: Origin and Future") Karl-Josef Kuschel astutely notes:

> In Abraham Jews, Christians, and Muslims have a unique orienting figure before them. ... From Abraham arise no claims to might among the religions. Abraham does not want to dominate. He opposes the aspiration to might, in general the strongest temptation of humankind. One who is on the way cannot wish to dominate. (Kuschel 2007, 621)

And in *Leben ist Brückenschlagen: Vordenker des interreligiösen Dialogs* ("To Live is to Build Bridges: Pathbreaking Thinkers of Interreligious Dialogue"), Kuschel adds that the underlying story told by his paradigmatic thinkers

> . . . shows that the future belongs not to the guardians of tradition but to the bold and spirited [*den Kühnen und Mutigen*]. It belongs to people who bring together what had been separated before, who travel paths of life that had hitherto been blocked. People, that is, who are capable of changes and further developments [*Entwicklungen*, literally "unfoldings"]. (Kuschel 2011, 16)

Thoughtful interpreters of Abraham, Feiler and Kuschel help empower me to write my dialogic books called "East-West Bridge Builders" (the book you are reading is Volume IV in the series; for the others see, in the Bibliography, Bidney 2009, Goethe 2010, Bidney 2013).

The presentation of Joseph in the Qur'an, an extended parable of pardon and compassion, is poetically remarkable to an unusual degree—not only for its own merits but because it would later generate, as well, outstanding Islamic narrative poems in a number of countries. The attempted seduction of Joseph by the wife of an Egyptian official, recounted in the Bible, is elaborated with vivid detail in the Qur'an. When the wife (traditionally called Zuleika or Zulaikha) is upbraided by her lady friends, she invites them to lunch to discuss the matter. She summons the ravishingly handsome Joseph, and the ladies are so unsettled by his beauty that they half-comically fumble with their fruit knives and cut their hands. Joseph, embarrassed, meanwhile hopes the enforced appearance will soon be terminated so he can return, with relief, to jail and be free of self-justifying seductresses (12:30–33, poem 42). Zuleika is summoned by her husband Aziz (the official, called Potiphar in the Bible), and Zuleika admits her wrongdoing. Joseph, having impressed Aziz, will now be made his right-hand man (12:51–54, poem 43).

My favorite part of the Qur'anic Joseph story centers on the reuniting, reconciling potential of his miracle-shirt. Zuleika has torn it from behind when pursuing him, and this fact is adduced to prove he was not the tempter, as Zuleika had desperately alleged, but rather her unwilling, resistant prey. When Joseph pardons his brothers their original abduction and abandonment of him, giving them ample stores of food to take back to the home of his beloved father Jacob, he also tells the brothers to take with them the shirt that had helped save him from Zuleika's wiles, and to lay it over Jacob's eyes. Jacob had cried himself blind with grief over his vanished son. The shirt, we now learn, will restore his vision. Indeed, Jacob, who has inner, prophetic sight as well as heightened senses enabling him to detect the shirt's fragrant aroma at a distance, already intuits that something wondrous will occur (12:93–6, poem 44).

When I taught for a month in Egypt (mid-January to mid-February 2011, which happened to be the time the anti-Mubarak revolution took place) at Sekem, an eco-sustainable desert settlement about an hour's ride from Cairo, my students, English teachers at the settlement school, spoke enthusiastically of the shirt of Joseph. They had never heard of his many-colored coat, mentioned in the Bible but not in the Qur'an. In the U.S., no non-Muslim I talked to had ever heard of the shirt, though they all knew the coat. Intercultural scripture reading, it would seem, can enrich the imaginations of us all. I loved having the chance to bring Bible and Qur'an together during my month of teaching and was touched when one student asked me, "Which is your favorite sura?" A hard choice. But, as a nighttime worker, I'm partial to "The Enshrouded One," where Allah says to the Prophet, "For We shall charge thee with a word of weight. Lo! the vigil of the night is (a time) when impression is more keen and speech more certain . . ." (73:5–6, poems 33, 127).

But the transcendent story of Joseph is not yet complete—not, at least, for admirers of Islamic verse. When Zuleika says, "I do not exculpate myself. Lo! the (human) soul enjoineth unto evil, save that whereon my Lord hath mercy. Lo! my Lord is Forgiving, Merciful" (12:53, poem 45), her words bear a fertile seed for literary imaginers. The word for "soul" here, *nafs* (related to Hebrew *nefesh*), traditionally signifies the lower soul, the weaker part subject to temptation. Because she renounces with such fervor the part of her that allowed itself to be led astray, Zuleika became, in the minds of many, a symbol of the soul repentant, rejecting its weaker part and ready to serve Allah in truth. As the legend continues to develop, she meets Joseph after her husband has died, and falls in love with him. One variant of the tale explains that Aziz had been impotent all along, thus leaving her chaste for Joseph. When Zuleika and Joseph are married, the redeemed soul is wedded to its ideal.

Few non-Muslim readers of the Bible would ever have imagined that the briefly recounted episode of Joseph and the Egyptian official's (former) wife had the potential to become one of the great love stories in world literature. Reading *Yusuf and Zulaikha: A Poem by Jami* (1414–1492) in the skillful 1882 verse translation by Ralph T. H. Griffith, we enjoy what many consider the finest of the surprisingly abundant re-envisionings. As regards the general impression we get of Joseph in the Qur'an, the gift of the shirt that restored his father's vision not only affirms his probity but amplifies a feature of his character that we earlier had learned of from the Bible: loving kindness. I will be returning to the theme that love is the unifying moral light of the Qur'an.

Our knowledge of Moses, David, and Solomon is comparably deepened by distinctively Qur'anic utterances and episodes that are ideal texts for tradition-unifying poetic homilies of compassionate love. When Moses returns from the mountain where he had received the Law, only to encounter the lawless worship of the golden calf, even though he is angry and grieved he immediately begs that the Lord have mercy on those led astray (7:151, poem 34). If the story of Moses' encounter with God speaking from the burning bush is retold in a manner readily recognizable to Bible readers (20:8–14, poem 62), the touchingly written two-part narrative of the Pharaoh's wife is a strikingly beautiful non-Biblical narrative evincing a depth of loving empathy. When she first sees the Hebrew child, the Pharaoh's wife (traditionally called Asiya) foretells that he will be a comfort, a "consolation" for her, and must be granted special care. Then, in later years, evidently inspired by Moses both in this first encounter and afterward, she suddenly turns to the true God and begs him to deliver her from the Pharaoh (28:9, 66:11, poem 79). In yet another remarkable tale, recalling the Biblical Babel narrative, Pharaoh directs his vizier Haman to build a tower to lead him to the roads of heaven, where he might look upon the God of Moses, "though," as he adds, "verily I think him a liar" (40:36–37, poem 101). Ruin ensues, of course, and the lesson of love is implied by showing, in contrast, how the arrogant harm themselves.

The instructive and touching Qur'anic story of the litigants who came to King David with a quarrel about ewes cannot be found in the Bible, though it is akin in important ways to Nathan's parable told to David in II Samuel 12:1–10. David rightly finds fault with the man who, though he owned ninety-nine ewes, could not rest content until he had persuaded his brother to yield up the single ewe owned by the latter. Envious brothers who deny the rule of love recall Cain and Abel, and the greedy enterpriser maltreating a poor man whose property he wants will also bring to mind Ahab and the vineyard-owner Naboth, or—later—Goethe's Faust and the aged Baucis and Philemon (38:22–26, poems 97, 96). Another cautionary tale is that of King Solomon, the jinns, and the worm. Allah subjected the jinns or fiery spirits to the monarch's rule, but evidently he overworked them in the multitude of his construction projects, for they "despised" their "toil" and wished they had understood the symbol of the little worm or "creeping creature of the earth" which had come to gnaw the royal staff just before the ruler died (34:12–14, poems 87, 90). This fine parable of pride and fall through lack of mindfulness is only sketched, but the reader's imagination gladly fills in the gaps.

Jewish and Islamic traditions are united in the light of the Qur'an. We see that although the biblical narratives of David and Solomon in the Books of Samuel, Kings, and Chronicles appear neither in Pentateuch nor Psalms (the Jewish books explicitly acknowledged holy in Islam), beautiful tales closely allied to them in content and import are nonetheless featured in Qur'anic presentations. Allah also tells important tidings both of Jonah (37:139–148, poems 94, 95) and of Job (21:83, poem 34).

Christian and Islamic legacies are unified through the same inclusive receptivity. Mary, Jesus, and John the Baptist are all favored in the Qur'an with non-Biblical episodes that readily invite the lyrical responder to envision the unifying lesson of love. As Muhammad had been early orphaned (93:6, poem 137), he was grateful for the kindness of his foster mother: he has even averred, in a well-accredited *hadith* or memoir-narrative, that paradise is "beneath the feet of the mothers" (poems 79, 137). This thought resonates in the mind when one reads the dignified and beautiful non-biblical prayer that the baby Jesus uttered while still in the cradle, avowing that Allah has made him "dutiful toward her who bore me, and hath not made me arrogant, unblest" (19:32, poem 58). As in Christianity, the Qur'anic Mary is a virgin, and Jesus is begotten with the aid of the Spirit of God; the birth of John the Baptist, too, is a miracle, as in the Gospel of Luke (21:89–94, poem 64). The Qur'an offers a charming tale, found in an apocryphal narrative of the infancy of Jesus but not in the Bible: Jesus models a bird out of clay, breathes upon it, and off it flies! (5:110, poems 27, 26). Here we have a lighthearted, exultant symbol of the loving bestowal of life, as upon Adam in Eden. The parable is presented before Jesus' other lifegiving wonders: curing blindness, healing leprosy, raising the dead (5:110). In sum: for the reader of the Qur'an, both the Torah and the Gospel are a "guidance and a light" (5:44, 46, poem 1).

Of Muhammad's life the Qur'an says little, for the concern of this scripture, composed by Allah and not by His Prophet, is to convey the message from the one God relating to His unifying nature and to the need for a godly human life. But there are quick and vivid flashes of parable-insight, brief sketches or hints, which were to be developed and elaborated in *hadith* memoir narratives. I have referred to the Prophet's being early orphaned, and to his reading of the Qur'an on the Night of Power. An additional transforming experience appears in Allah's rescue of Muhammad and his friend Abu Bakr when they take shelter from their pursuers in a cave (9:40, poems 37, 113).

A deeply affecting episode of the Prophet's life is recounted in Sura 80:1–16, "'He Frowned'" (poems 130, 131). Here we learn that, trying to receive graciously a privileged and perhaps influential visitor, the Prophet neglected the simultaneous appeal of a blind man. The story is rightly praised as written on "honored leaves," and as "exalted" and "purified," not only because it is a cautionary parable from which we can learn alertness to the call of the disadvantaged, but also because, as both Allah and Muhammad wished, it helps us remember at all times that the latter is himself no god but only a messenger, a bearer of good tidings, not a "warder" over humankind but a "remembrancer" of a loving Creator (88:21, poem 47).

I will not be discussing the extra-Qur'anic narrative of the excision of the Prophet's heart by angels, the removal of a speck of imperfection that rightly belonged only to Satan, the covering of the heart with a cooling fluid, and the re-placing of it in his breast (hinted in 94:1–4). Also not studied in detail is the Prophet's lightning-swift journey from Mecca to Jerusalem on the back of the winged steed Buraq (hinted in 17:1, referenced in poems 20, 103, 140), or the Prophet's tour of the seven heavens after being purified to speak the word of God (sketched in 53:1–11). These memoir-narratives are explored in my earlier *East-West Poetry* (2009). Here we focus on lyrical responses to the Qur'an itself.

(5) Love as Unifying Moral Light:
Radiant States of Being and Modes of Loving Action

The serene joy in shared wonder that animates the Qur'an has moral implications, and the scripture gives plentiful guidance for an ethical life with oneself and others. The unifying moral light of the Qur'an is that of Love. Tthe love-imparting virtues embodied and prescribed in many Qur'anic passages that affect me deeply are *generosity, peace of mind, forgiveness,* and *stewardship*. All four of these states of mind and heart are *subsets of love*. They are at once virtues and rewards, the virtue being its own reward. All of them are best applied by combining the depth of an empathetic heart with the light of a discerning mind, exercising the alert attention that Buddhists call "mindfulness."

A special quality of the four virtues is that each is both a *state of being* and a *mode of action*. Any one of the radiant, loving states of being will predispose the soul to loving acts and will express it in kindly deeds. In the same way, the Light of the sun—which is a self-sufficient outward movement of particles and waves in rays—additionally warms, illuminates, and enlivens what it touches, uniting in this activity all creatures that are thus benignly affected. Generosity, peace of mind, forgiveness, and stewardship express *a unifying light,* as witnessed in a *radiant state of spirit,* and as manifested in *the grace of loving action.*

a) Generosity

A loving generosity is central to the religion that Muhammad explains in the Qur'an. Almsgiving or charity is one of the five pillars of Islam; the others are faith in God and in His Prophet; prayer; fasting in the month of Ramadan; and making a pilgrimage to Mecca. Many are the Qur'anic praises of spending in a caring way, many the castigations of selfish hoarding. Generosity of spirit is clarified and commended in one of the most perfectly wrought, well-pondered chapters of the Qur'an, Sura 93 "The Morning Hours" (93:5–11, poem 137):

> In the name of Allah, the Beneficent, the Merciful.
> 1. By the morning hours
> 2. And by the night when it is stillest,
> 3. Thy Lord hath not forsaken thee nor doth He hate thee,
> 4. And verily the latter portion will be better for thee than the former,
> 5. And verily thy Lord will give unto thee so that thou wilt be content.
> 6. Did He not find thee an orphan and protect (thee)?
> 7. Did He not find thee wandering and direct (thee)?
> 8. Did He not find thee destitute and enrich (thee)?
> 9. Therefor the orphan oppress not,
> 10. Therefor the beggar drive not away,
> 11. Therefor of the bounty of thy Lord be thy discourse.

In a word: "Feed with food the needy wretch, the orphan and the prisoner" (76:8).

There is more to say of generosity in the Qur'an, but I would like to digress for just a moment to comment on the vigor, majesty, and beauty of the sura we've just heard. Not a mere sermon, it is a work of poetic depth and skill: the initial two lines set the calming, illumined mood, and the stately rhythms mark the point at which rhetorical dexterity blends with spiritual depth. (I can't help but think here of Abraham Lincoln's Gettysburg Address, itself heavily indebted to the rhetorical poetry of scripture, and embodying the same generosity of heart as in the sura.) A fine translation, one that speaks to the heart and mind at once, may not have the same beauty as the original, but yet can be beautiful *differently,* and not unworthily. Such a differently-beautiful attempt to render the same lyrical sura is the highly unusual one by Friedrich Rückert in German (see Alam, *Gottespoesie*), which seeks to duplicate not only the strong rhythms of the original but even its multiple rhymes, as I'll try to show now by rendering it in English:

1. By the day that will rise!
2. And by night, silent-wise!
3. The Lord has abandoned you not, nor yet ever denies.
4. Beyond is more than one here espies.
5. More riches will He grant than you can realize.
6. Were you not found by Him an orphan, and then nourished?
7. A wanderer, then led and cherished?
8. A needy one, then fed, to flourish?
9. The orphan decry not,
10. The beggar deny not,
11. Proclaim your Maker's grace!

Rückert's rendering of the *Koran* is not quite complete, but it is superb. I wanted to include a sample to suggest how deeply melodious the many-rhymed Arabic recitation (which we hear in the chantings on internet) must be for the speaker of that language.

To resume our theme of the centrality of generosity for Islamic faith and action: "The likeness of those who spend their wealth in Allah's way is as the likeness of a grain which groweth seven ears, in every ear an hundred grains" (2:261, poem 16). To spend wealth in Allah's way is to satisfy the needs of the orphan, the beggar, the destitute. Another likeness to the righteous way of spending is that of a "garden on a height" (2:265, poem 17), dispensing bounty as the Lord did to Muhammad. Generosity of spirit in the way of the Lord is commended with vigor: "Those who spend their wealth by night and day, by stealth and openly, verily their reward is with their Lord, and there shall no fear come upon them neither shall they grieve" (2:274, poems 6, 7, 8, 18).

To expend energy and wealth in good works is to surrender the selfhood. Abundance of spirit means we quell the willful, selfish ego: "Whosoever surrendereth his purpose to Allah while doing good, he verily hath grasped the firm hand-hold" (31:22, poem 82). Those who "spend of that We have bestowed on them" have an incalculable reward (32:16–17, poem

84); they "look forward to imperishable gain" (35:29, poem 92). The time to give abundantly is now, not later (63:10, poem 120). For "whoso is saved from his own greed, such are the successful" (64:16, poems 121, 122). To succeed is to radiate the light of generosity—to spend, not hoard.

b) Peace of Mind

Peace of mind—equanimity, tranquillity, serenity—includes a group of related virtues: modesty, patience, restraint, dignity of demeanor, and respect for dignity in others. The "peace of reassurance," coming down from Allah, may be supported by "hosts ye cannot see" (9:26, 40, poem 37). One feels a tranquil solace in Allah's cheering counsel to the heavy-laden: ". . . lo! with hardship goeth ease, Lo! with hardship goeth ease!" (94:5–6, poems 138, 139). The greeting of the righteous souls in the Eden of the afterlife will be "Peace"; the "word of a Merciful Lord (for them) is: Peace!" (14:23, 36:67, poem 39). So Allah urges us here on earth: ". . . ah! thou soul at peace! Return unto thy Lord, content in His good pleasure" (89:27–28, poem 45). Jesus, known to the Christian as the Prince of Peace, is confirmed in this character by the Qur'an when in his cradle he prays, "Peace on me the day I was born, and the day I die, and the day I shall be raised alive!" (19:33, poems 57, 58). In the Heavenly Eden one hears "no idle talk, but only Peace," and this will be "food for morn and evening" (19:62, poem 60, and see the note by A. Yusuf Ali on the sixfold meaning of salām or peace). The righteous who "were stedfast" will meet in heaven "with welcome and the word of peace" (25:75, poems 68, 73). The scornful man, the braggart, is told to "be modest and subdue thy voice. Lo! the harshest of all voices is the voice of the ass" (31:18–19, poem 82); dignity and equanimity modestly renounce overbearing pride—but not humor.

Braggadocio and swagger indicate mental insecurity—the opposite of the peace of mind praised in the Qur'an. When braggarts claim, "We are more (than you) in wealth and children" or "We are not the punished" (34:35, poem 91), they penalize themselves through isolation from their fellows. Entry into the tranquillity of Eden is secured by "a contrite heart" (50:31–33, poem 111; cf. Psalm 34:18, Isaiah 57:15, 66:2). Supreme peace of mind was God's gift to Muhammad during the momentous time of the Great Recital, the reading of the Qur'an on the Night of Power: "(That night is) Peace until the rising of the dawn" (97:5, poem 140).

Peace of mind will be both cause and consequence of a high regard for our neighbor's freedom of moral choice. Allah unmistakably proclaims, "There is no compulsion in religion" (2:256, poems 14, 15). When Adam and Eve go astray, God quickly relents: freedom understandably may lead to error. As I phrase it in poem 6, "Deflection is a lesser deed / Of ill than hate would be" but nonetheless a moral problem. "Allah is the Relenting, the Merciful" (2:37), for He understands how crucial is our mental freedom from compulsion. Moreover, those who worry that the self-esteem of the Divinity would be injured by a slight are rebuked: "Lo! those who disbelieve and turn from the way of Allah and oppose the messenger after the guidance hath been manifested unto them, they hurt Allah not a jot" (47:32, poem 106). God, Who is Absolute Mind and Heart, is not damaged by the denials of a skeptic: He is bigger than that. Ebusu'ud wrote a *fatwa* advising an inquirer who wanted to censor a poet's work for blasphemy that this would be a waste of effort (epigraph to poem 106). A mind at peace will not seek to compel. It will "shun much suspicion" (49:12, poem 109). The rule of "no compulsion" leads to equanimity—harmony within the mind and with the world.

Finally, peace of mind will make you patient and understanding. We need to pacify wrath (poem 99), but also to quell overeagerness. God warns Muhammad to "hasten not . . . with the Qur'ân ere its revelation hath been perfected unto thee" (20:114, poem 63). The Prophet must learn patience, and so must we all: "if he remain patient, verily it is better for the patient" (16:126, poem 52). Peace of mind will grant the strength of patience to the tranquil person, as when Allah tells the Prophet to "bear with patience" the jibes of importunate skeptics, to "part from them with a fair leave-taking," and to "respite them awhile" (73:10–11, poem 127). He adds, ". . . be patient (O Muhammad) with a patience fair to see" (70:5, poems 124, 125). Equanimity is not easy to attain, but great is the reward (32:15–17, poem 84). The problem, the obstacle, goes deeper than one might think: "Man prayeth for evil as he prayeth for good, for man was ever hasty" (17:11, poem 52). Patient understanding depends on a contemplative, embracing awareness, a calm and empathetic observation of the mutual complementarity of contraries (53: 43–45, poem 53). It is a mild, embracing light.

c) Forgiveness

The central position of Forgiveness, including the related merit of compassionate mercy and closely linked, as well, to the patience that comes from peace of mind, is formulated by Allah in a clear and forthright way: "And verily whoso is patient and forgiveth—lo! That, verily, is (of) the stedfast heart of things" (42:43, poem 105). Pardon is of the heart, the core, the central nature of the spirit that is generous, tranquil, and radiant. Mercy informs the pre-emptive pardon that God Himself practices, and it does this in a reassuring way when He "tasketh not a soul beyond its scope" (2:286, poems 19, 20), compassionately understanding the limitations of us all. Allah offers implicit pardon to humans when he relents after the fall of Adam and Eve (2:37, poems 6, 7). God, showing "vast mercy" (53:32, poem 112), sent Muhammad "as a mercy for the peoples" (21:107, poem 65), and we should follow that example of kindness by heeding the maxim, "Repel evil with that which is better" (23:96, poem 44). A variant of the maxim urges: "Repel the evil deed with one which is better," and then "he, between whom and thee there was enmity (will become) as though he were a bosom friend" (41:34, poem 102). Repaying ill with good turns hate to love.

Says Muhammad to His Lord, "Thou art best of all who show mercy" (23:118, poem 34), and Allah in turn urges, "So forgive, O Muḥammad, with a gracious forgiveness" (15:85, poem 47), even as Abraham begged that pardon might be extended toward his erring father (26:86, poems 74, 75). David judged rightly with regard to the man greedy for ewes, and when for unknown causes even this prudent decision aroused in David the acknowledgment of a hidden guilt, the Lord nonetheless duly forgave him the enigmatic trespass (38:26, poem 97). A rhapsodic upburst in the Qur'an exults in wonderment respecting the heaven-shaking drama of pardon: "Almost might the heavens above be rent asunder while the angels hymn the praise of their Lord and ask forgiveness for those on the earth. Lo! Allah is the Forgiver, the Merciful" (42:5, poem 103). Exhilarating, too, is the way the competitive urge that we feel can be sublimated to the level of a lofty virtue, not a destructive rivalry but the acceptance of a welcome challenge and a high resolve: "Race with one another for forgiveness from your Lord and a Garden whereof the breadth is as the breadth of the heavens and the earth" (57:21, poem 137).

d) Stewardship

The fourth and final crucial virtue taught in the Qur'anic passages I love best is Stewardship, or "Trust." It is an overarching, loving light that can unify us, in care and understanding, with our dwelling place, our planet, our uni- and pluriverse. The central saying for our Earth today is this one: "Lo! We offered the trust unto the humans and the earth and the hills, but they sank from bearing it and were afraid of it. And man assumed it. Lo! He hath proved a tyrant and a fool" (33:72, poems 5, 87, 88, 89). "Trust," *amāna* (compare Hebrew *emunāh*, "faithfulness"), is something humans agreed to. It is a responsibility that we alone bear consciously among created beings. Allah deplores that we have ignored our singular accountability, neglected our acknowledged role to work for the welfare of earth. Remarkably, though, Allah still believes in us. For He writes: "And when thy Lord said unto the angels: Lo! I am about to place a viceroy in the earth, they said: Wilt Thou place therein one who will do harm therein and will shed blood, while we, we hymn Thy praise and sanctify Thee? He said: Surely I know that which ye know not" (2:30, poem 5). What does Allah perceive in us that the angels cannot? Is it our capacity to behold a unifying light?

The angels foresaw our planetary negligence, our potential for carnage, destruction, and the debasement of our dwelling place. But Allah retains a trust—in us!—though we are now the proven tyrants of the planet. Our technologically empowered devastations are prefigured by the way King Solomon overdrove the jinns to construct massive architectural and industrial works, "basins like wells and boilers built into the ground" (34:13, poem 87). But the natural landscape offers a healthy balance we should not wantonly destroy. "And He hath cast into the earth firm hills that it quake not with you, and streams and roads that ye may find a way" (16:15, poem 48). All forms of life contribute to the well-being of the world. "There is not an animal in the earth, nor a flying creature flying on two wings, but they are peoples like unto you. We have neglected nothing in the Book (of Our decrees) . . ." (6:38, poem 29).

In fancied human superiority we leave unregarded our fellow "peoples" of the animal realm. They do not evade their obligations but fulfill them unawares. We alone were offered "trust" or stewardship of the planet as something to be consciously attained with steadfast work and planning (poem 88). God sent the Prophet to the world in mercy, and He is saddened that we have shown so little mercy to our home, which would otherwise become an Eden for us and our fellow Garden-dwellers (33:72). The faith in us that Allah still maintains (2:30) is a wonder, a stimulus, and a hope. It should inspire us to work hard, and quickly. For "man hath only that for which he maketh effort" (53:39, poem 113). And effort will be rewarded, as God has affirmed in breathtaking poetry (84:16–19, poem 132):

> Oh, I swear by the afterglow of sunset,
> And by the night and all that it enshroudeth,
> And by the moon when she is at the full,
> That ye shall journey on from plane to plane.

Plenitude is height, for transcendences converge, and lights will unify.

(6) Influences from Islamic Tradition and Elsewhere

I conclude with notes on the books and people, Islamic and other, that have influenced my Qur'an-stimulated lyrical presentation of the embracing light. The Sufi poetry of the *Divan* (Collection) by Hafiz (ca. 1320–1390), rendered into German by Joseph von Hammer in the edition that stimulated Goethe to write his *West-East Divan*, has aided my understanding of the Qur'an. In Hammer II.231–2 Mim 50 we find a poem (see Bidney, 2013, 138) containing these lines:

> Answer me, Lord, when I ask: what am I destined to be?
> I, when a servant, devoted, the tavern of love was frequénting—
>   Nothing but burdens anew daily a visit would bring.
> Heart's-blood has reddened my eyes—and my wildness the least of my worries.
>   Fool to surrender my heart!—why did I give it to *them*?
> Writ on its tablet is only the "one" of my Friend, letter *álif*.
>   That's what my Master had taught; nothing more wise could I know!

I elaborate this theme: the single stroke of the first letter of the Arabic alphabet is the Beginning, the Origin, the mark of Allah graven on the heart (poems 2, 100, 133). Shahid Alam has created a sculpture of the *álif* (back cover of this book) that is akin to Brancusi's *Bird in Flight*.

Rumi (1207–1273), another Sufi master, more mystical than Hafiz, influenced me more deeply still. I borrow his metaphor of God as dyeing vat (poem 10) and allude to his likening of the universe to a vast dancing fire (poem 41). I add Rumi's speculation that each of is a *zarra*, or atom-like mote, ecstatically dancing in that single cosmic flame-whirl (poems 117, 128). I reference Mevlana Rumi's founding of the Mevlevi order of whirling dervishes (poem 66), cite his likeness of the dervish flute to the reed's longing for her home in the marsh (poem 123), and bring in the flute music that accompanies dervish dancing in Turkey yet today (poem 134). Rabi'a, a saintly Sufi woman of Islam who died in the year 801, appears in a heavenly exaltation analogous to the aura of the Queen of Sheba for King Solomon (poem 77).

The Sufi tendency in Qur'anic interpretation is introspective, mystical, and searchingly imaginative. I have read so much about it in the wondrously learned books of Annemarie Schimmel (who also edited a volume to honor Rückert, *Weltpoesie ist Weltversöhnung*, "World Poetry is World Conciliation") and in the widely-studied book *The Sufis* by Idries Shah that often I can no longer recall the particular Sufi master to be credited with a particular insight. Shahid Alam, calligrapher and artist, has conveyed to me additional Sufi teachings. You will find Sufi themes in a number of my lyrics. I introduce a thought on the value of "not-knowing" that I acquired from the just-mentioned book by Idries Shah which I consulted often while in Egypt (poem 15). Shahid Alam had told me that his Sufi grandmother had blessed him by saying inaudibly a sacred word, then softly breathing onto him; and you will find here a visitant houri, or supernatural emissary-maiden, offering a blessing through "on-breathing" (poem 15). Later, I recall Shahid's delightful Sufi intimation that a tree grows from above (poem 100), and I thankfully transmit the Sufi wisdom that we should be grateful for our gratitude (poem 76). I have already cited the Sufi idea that the Qur'an text read by the Prophet may have been written in the immaterial heart of the universe (poem 116). Such an insight is corroborated by the vast treasury of Sufi translations, expositions, and clear, vigorous analyses offered by William C. Chittick; I had only begun to sample these while writing the present book (see his *Divine Love* in the Bibliography). Poet Omar Khayyám, deemed a Sufi by some, and known widely in the Victorian *Rubáiyát* rendering by Edward FitzGerald, provided the stanza form—with rhyme pattern *aaxa, bbxb*—that I modify to *aaba, bbcb* in many of my own lyrics (e.g., poems 3, 5, 20, 22, 96, 100, 110 part 2, 112, 125, 134, 137, 140, "Concluding Thought" part 1) or to *aaba ccbc* (poems 6, 30).

Muhammad praised the blessed diversity of our world (10:20, 35:27–28, 49:13), and a well-known *hadith* cites the Prophet's recommendation to seek knowledge wherever it may be found, "even though it be in China." So, just as in *East-West Poetry* I offered lyrics with such titles as "Allah and Buddha," or "Rumi and Hegel," here I similarly seek for intercultural wealth of spirit. The word "mindfulness," used earlier, derives from my study of Buddhism, and so does the Japanese term "satori," indicating the moment of illumination (poems 32, 70, 107). In this book you will find an allusion to a Hindu meditative technique. AUM (simplified often to OM) emblemizes the Unity of Being in the exterior world (A) and the interior one (U), bridged by the central linking letter (M), which may signify the meditation that brings the two together. We also unite the inner and outer worlds in pondering Hafiz' idea of the *álif*, the Arabic alpha written in a single stroke (indicating the origin and source of Being in Allah), which is graven on our hearts.

Western influences, ancient and modern, have helped me. The beautiful Qur'an parable of Jesus making a bird of clay brought to mind, in poem 26, the *boustróphedon* method of writing that I heard about when visiting the Greek Islands, a forward-and-backward alternating direction of lines, following the plowman's path. So I wrote the poem in a Greek meter, the third asclepiadic (learned from the Roman Hellenophile Horace). I use another Grecian rhythm pattern, the dactylic hexameter, the meter of Homer, in the epigraph and the reply of poem 51 where I translate (from a German version) part of a Kallimachos ode about bees and honey, relating to Sura 16 "The Bee." I used the elegiac (Theocritan, Ovidian) couplet or distich, as Joseph Hammer did in German, to render the Hafiz lines quoted above (p. xliii).

Seventeenth-century philosopher Baruch Spinoza is featured, along with Matthew and Luke, to reinforce the moral emphasized and repeated in the Qur'an: "Repel evil with that which is better (23:96); "Repel the evil deed with one which is better" 41:34, poem 69). William Blake's "Auguries of Innocence" are invoked (poem 46), and the Goethean write-up of Mejnun and Laila, the Romeo and Juliet of medieval Persia, in lyric 79 of his *West-East Divan* (poem 67). Goethe's *Divan* translation of a fatwa by Ebusu'ud is referenced in the epigraph to poem 106. Among modern influences I may cite Ernst Kris, psychoanalyst of creative artists (poem 26), and Russian literary critic Mikhail Bakhtin, who not only gave me the word "chronotope," or "timeplace" (poem 19) but, more important, has provided in several classic works a model of the "dialogic" thinking that motivates me to write. A wise and helpful Turkish tour guide, Semih Eser, provided the legend of Mehmet II and the repositioned mosque (poem 11). He told me, too, of the reputed piety of storks, who nest in minarets and cry "Lak, lak!" or "Yours, Yours!" (poem 82).

For the illustrations I thank artist Shahid Alam, my friend and mentor in Islamic and Sufi thought. With Dr. Ibrahim Abouleish, founder of the eco-sustainable Sekem settlement in Egypt, I have discussed the Abrahamic religions' three orienting texts, and he invited me to a Sekem ceremony involving a recitation of these to celebrate the harmony of the three traditions, just as Shahid Alam displays the texts in Arabic on tablets at his intercultural exhibitions of calligraphic painting and sculpture in the city halls, churches, and cathedrals of Germany. And I am endlessly indebted to Katharina Mommsen, Professor Emerita at Stanford University—teacher, counselor, colleague, and friend—who commented on most of the poems of this book, and whose correspondence with me, symbolically indicated here by epigraphs from her letters (poems 30, 123), has been a fountain of intellectual strength and unfailing vigor. Her pioneering books *Goethe und die arabische Welt* (1988) and *Goethe und der Islam* (2001) have shaped my East-West outlook. I thank Johanna Masters and Anni Johnson for reading many of my Qur'anic poems, and to Anni for listening to me read the "Introduction" two times aloud and offering sage advice. She even suggested the title *A Unifying Light*. To Sheryl Rowe of Bytheway Publishing Services I owe deepest gratitude for her efficient and tasteful formatting and typesetting.

Finally, a word about the Pickthall translation of the Qu'an. Taking scholarly care to ensure philological accuracy by putting all interpretive material in parentheses to distinguish it from the rendering of words present in the Arabic text, Pickthall is at the same time a singer at heart. During his youth in England, before he converted to Islam as an adult, Pickthall may well have heard and absorbed the cadences of the Authorized Version of the Bible (1611), a towering masterwork of the English language. The phrasing of his Qur'an has a seventeenth-century directness, vigor, strength, and majesty recalling the golden age of Shakespeare, Donne, Burton, Browne. When God says to Muhammad, "Remind them, for thou art but a remembrancer, Thou art not at all a warder over them" (63:21–22), the words "remembrancer" and "warder" come across with archaic resonance and power. When in *East-West Poetry* I used as a refrain the line "A warder art thou not, but a remembrancer," my alexandrine, or iambic hexameter line, rose up by itself from the vibrant Pickthall text. In the present book, Abraham's prayer (26:83–89, poem 75) and God's words to Jonah (37:139–148, poem 94) are almost, respectively, seven-beat and six-beat poems already, and my metrically regular opening strophes alter the Qur'anic passages only slightly. When quoting, I maintain Pickthall's unusual spellings "therefor" and "stedfast," and when writing I make liberal use of his pungent, colorful vocabulary, including "froward," meaning "self-willed, intractable." I hope to begin a tradition of Qur'an-based English-language poetry stimulated by the achievement of Marmaduke Pickthall.

1.
Lyrical Response to Sura 1 "The Opening," Verses in Sura 5 "The Table Spread"

In the name of Allah, the Beneficent, the Merciful,
1:1. Praise be to Allah, Lord of the Worlds,
2. The Beneficent, the Merciful.
3. Owner of the Day of Judgment,
4. Thee (alone) we worship; Thee (alone) we ask for help.
5. Show us the straight path,
6. The path of those whom Thou hast favoured;
7. Not (the path) of those who earn Thine anger nor of those who go astray.

5:44. Lo! We did reveal the Torah, wherein is guidance and a light. . . .
46. We bestowed on him [Jesus] the Gospel wherein is guidance and a light. . . .
48. . . . And unto thee [O Muhammad] have We revealed the Scripture with the truth, confirming whatever Scripture was before it, and a watcher over it.

> The "Hear, O Israel" and "Our Father" if we place
> Together with "The Opening," we then may see
> How Islam, Judaism, Christianity
> Are gems whereof the radiances interlace.
>
> The origin to Father Abraham we trace
> Of this tradition. Here the Lord portrayed the three
> As light and guidance. If we'd well instructed be,
> We'll hymn the glory limned in every jewel-face.
>
> Now to "The Opening" we'll open our embrace:
> A mirrored mutual illumination we
> Are ready to receive in token of the grace
>
> That lent to ages depth from where, resplendently,
> The strength outspread to fill with life the heaven-space
> In mercy to the world of time-eternity.

2.
Lyrical Response to the Title of Sura 1 "The Opening"

In the name of Allah, the Beneficent, the Merciful,
1. Praise be to Allah, Lord of the Worlds,
2. The Beneficent, the Merciful.
3. Owner of the Day of Judgment,
4. Thee (alone) we worship; Thee (alone) we ask for help.
5. Show us the straight path,
6. The path of those whom Thou hast favoured;
7. Not (the path) of those who earn Thine anger nor of those who go astray.

The *álif,* Arab alphabetic opening,
Is the beginning of the holy writing art.
So Háfiz claimed that God engraved upon his heart
The single upright stroke to emblem Heaven's King.

Now babies' antenatal curled positioning
Precedes the vertical, erect, or opened-out:
The human hand, as well, as if in womb-redoubt,
Will make a fist at rest—an apt symbolic thing

A friend had told me, who's a carpal therapist.
The hand, when open and extended, shapes a line
Preparing for creation, making by design.

The darkness in the middle of the rounded fist
We then release, and Allah's *álif*-hand will shine—
The light it knows to hail is Maker, the Divine.

3.
Lyrical Response to Verses in Sura 1 "The Opening"

In the name of Allah, the Beneficent, the Merciful.
1. Praise be to Allah, Lord of the Worlds,
2. The Beneficent, the Merciful.
3. Owner of the Day of Judgment,
4. Thee (alone) we worship; Thee (alone) we ask for help. . . .

        The mercy-dew outpoured, unspent,
        Upon Your creature new-besprent,
        I'm hoping for, in May awaked,
        As for a heaven-element.

        The liquid-craving bloom, unslaked
        In thirst for dewburst, long had ached:
        The burning of her heart a song
        Had tried to milden. Rain-unstraked,

        Unaided I, O make me strong
        Who as by cymbal, bell, or gong
        Am called to chant the world aware
        Of Maker-strength a summer long.

        Throughout unending fields of air
        I'd will to send my feeling, where
        The littlest atom yet unlent
        To singer-bliss I'd glad prepare.

4.
Lyrical Response to a Verse in Sura 2 "The Cow"

25. And give glad tidings (O Muhammad) unto those who believe and do good works; that theirs are Gardens underneath which rivers flow; as often as they are regaled with food of the fruit thereof, they say: This is what was given us aforetime; and it is given to them in resemblance. . . .

    What's granted us in heaven but a kind resemblance
    Of what we loved on earth and held in prized remembrance,
    Continued in imagination unabating?
    I'm feeling more than thinking, playing more than stating . . .
    By this I mean: from deepest ground to highest heaven
    I levitated seem when lent melodic leaven—

    By music overswept with purifying breeze—
    Within the holy moment, the beholder sees.
    Who heard the chanting of the Allah Scripture first,
    Entranced in raptured gladness, were trans-universed.
    To laud the living-gift, elating one who praised,
    Will make him feel on earth to higher light upraised.

5.
Lyrical Response to Verses in Suras 2 "The Cow," 33 "The Clans"

2:30. And when thy Lord said unto the angels: Lo! I am about to place a viceroy in the earth, they said: Wilt Thou place therein one who will do harm therein and will shed blood, while we, we hymn Thy praise and sanctify Thee? He said: Surely I know that which ye know not.

142. . . . He guideth whom He will unto a straight path.

33:72. Lo! We offered the trust unto the heavens and the earth and the hills, but they shrank from bearing it and were afraid of it. And man assumed it. Lo! He hath proved a tyrant and a fool.

> A tyrant and a fool has Adam proved, and yet
> For viceroy in the earth a God, prophetic, set
> This being whom the angels trembled when they saw,
> Foreseeing evil that the creature would beget.
>
> Too deep for tears the word (I'm hearing it with awe)
> Wherein the Lord implies that man to higher law
> Will be compliant in a mode He best will know:
> In Him we see how faith can blest connection draw.
>
> Yes, God believed in us! and told the angel so.
> The *álif* that He drew upon your heart would show
> The straight and upright path to which He'd wisely guide
> The all-too-strong and wide astray, who'd righteous grow
>
> If they by loving intimation might abide
> And so convinced, convicted, quickly throw aside
> Unholy, bloated ego, self-indulgent fret—
> For dreadful is the woe of titans in their pride.

6.
Lyrical Response to Verses in Sura 2 "The Cow"

35. And We said: O Adam! Dwell thou and thy wife in the Garden, and eat ye freely (of the fruits) thereof where ye will; but come not nigh this tree lest ye become wrongdoers.
36. But Satan caused them to deflect therefrom and expelled them from the (happy) state in which they were. . . .
37. Then Adam received from his Lord words (of revelation), and He relented toward him. Lo! He is the Relenting, the Merciful.
39. We said: Go down, all of you, from hence; but verily there cometh unto you from Me a guidance; and whoso followeth My guidance, there shall no fear come upon them neither shall they grieve.

Command was given, followed not:
What Adam, Eve, and Satan wrought
In triple failure to obey
Would cause a lesson to be taught.

The narrative is told with speed:
Deflection is a lesser deed
Of ill than hate would be. So pay
To His relenting guidance heed.

No fear will come; they shall not grieve
Who in the Merciful believe.
Deserving of high praise are they
Whom Satan can't of kindness thieve.

And how shall loving flourish, then?
You must relent, relent again.
No evil can the heart affray
That rule of lenitude will ken.

7.
Lyrical Response to Verses in Sura 2 "The Cow"

35. And We said: O Adam! Dwell thou and thy wife in the Garden, and eat ye freely (of the fruits) thereof where ye will; but come not nigh this tree lest ye become wrongdoers.

36. But Satan caused them to deflect therefrom and expelled them from the (happy) state in which they were; and We said: Fall down, one of you a foe unto the other! There shall be for you on earth a habitation and provision for a time.

37. Then Adam received from his Lord words (of revelation), and He relented toward him. Lo! He is the Relenting, the Merciful.

38. We said: Go down, all of you, from hence; but verily there cometh unto you from Me a guidance; and whoso followeth My guidance, there shall no fear come upon them neither shall they grieve.

    We said to Eve and Adam, Dwell
    In Eden, and content you well
    With all the fruitage meant for you:
    From but one tree avert your view.
    But Satan lent the two unease
    'Mid such approved amenities:
    They fell in ugly struggle, foes
    Till Allah should a cure disclose.

    When Adam readily had heard
    The needed revelation-word,
    It showed the Lord relented, Who
    Will judge—but cure in Mercy, too:
    The ones who hear the Lord may know
    A soul at ease—and forward go
    Assured that never fear will thieve
    Their freedom; neither shall they grieve.

    No derogated wayward Eve,
    No snake wherein we need believe,
    No heritable taint of sin,
    Benightedness, or blight within . . .

Our parable-similitude
With kinder light we find endued:
A braver tune may indicate
We view, more plainly, heaven-gate.

8.
Lyrical Response to Verses in Suras 2 "The Cow," 5 "The Table Spread"

2:62. Lo! those who believe (in that which is revealed unto thee, Muhammad), and those who are Jews, and Christians, and Sabaeans—whoever believeth in Allah and the Last Day and doeth right—surely their reward is with their Lord, and there shall no fear come upon them neither shall they grieve.

5:68. Say, O People of the Scripture! Ye have naught (of guidance) till ye observe the Torah and the Gospel and that which was revealed unto you from your Lord. . . .
69. Lo! Those who believe, and those who are Jews, and Sabaeans, and Christians—Whosoever believeth in Allah and the Last Day and doeth right—there shall no fear come upon them neither shall they grieve.

> No fear shall come upon them, neither shall they grieve—
> Sabaean, Jew, and Christian—who what they believe
> Shall manifest in kindness, doing what is right;
> Qur'an, Toráh, and Gospel grant a holy light.
>
> On loved, well-thumbed Qur'an I knew the cover, green,
> The Prophet's color, told of hope in shade pristine:
> That Primal solitude might yield to harmony,
> The One created two, for You require a me.
>
> The ones who fear and sorrow trigger so bereave
> The peaceful of the love that's due them as to thieve
> A sacred soul, God's making, of a depth and height
> Perfused with mildened rays in full celestial might.
>
> Qur'an, Toráh, and Gospel, and Sabaean books,
> And others that we know not of—whoever looks
> Upon their leaves for green, the hue of hope in heart,
> Will brightest guidance of the Lord on High impart.

9.
Lyrical Response to a Verse in Sura 2 "The Cow"

74. Then . . . hearts were hardened and became as rocks, or worse than rocks, for hardness. For indeed there are rocks from out which rivers gush, and indeed there are rocks which split asunder so that water floweth from them. And indeed there are rocks which fall down for the fear of Allah.

A guide in flexibility of metaphor,
In open-hearted skill and wide, receptive mind,
Is here, a mentor-thought, a source that can restore
Imaginative strength, and fetters taut unbind
So that the God-empowered, liberated mind
Will empathy in kinship find and, flying, soar.

The rock: mere hardness? No, from stone a river flows
In gushing, urgent, downward drive; or waters climb
By impulse underground upthrown, that might unclose
A rill that Moses would in trance behold sublime;
And fated rockfalls may recall the paradigm
Of awed prostration as when wind through reed-field goes.

From what is often taken for an emblem cold
Of obduracy, adamantine stubbornness,
We make a threefold symbol of a triply bold
Metáphorizing will to foster and to bless:
In loving, humble poetry of high largesse
A thought of death is turned to those that life will hold.

The upthrust of a river, spring that from a stone
Arose, and the descent of boulders from a height
Are images of what the poetry alone
Of depth or heaven, both alike in bearing light,
May offer to the wise, a land-enchanting might
Through fliers only found who bounds have overflown.

10.
Lyrical Response to a Verse in Sura 2 "The Cow"

138. (We take our) colour from Allah, and who is better than Allah at colouring. We are his worshippers.

        Rumi pictured God as dyeing vat.
        Soul, the garment dipped therein, would be
        Bathed in all-including whiteness that
        Blended tints in His Infinity:
        Cleansed of all iniquity would we
        Radiant gleam, the angels glad thereat.

        Poets, Lord-devoted, never war
        Over choice of images that they
        May select for holy metaphor,
        Make them dance in grand, accordant play.
        Many's the imaginative way
        We the greatness of the Grace adore.

        Let me then suggest the emblem true
        While we dwell on earth had best be green.
        So, rejoicing, Adam, Eve would view
        Trees of Life: each leaf as symbol seen
        Of a Stewardship that, pure, serene,
        Can preserve a world of heightened hue.

11.
Lyrical Response to a Verse in Sura 2 "The Cow"

142. The foolish of the people will say: What hath turned them from the qiblah which they formerly observed? Say: Unto Allah belong the East and the West. He guideth whom He will unto a straight path.

Qíblah, the direction that we face
When we pray, the Lord had altered so
Mecca, not Jerusalem, the place
Now would be to which the word will go.
Changes are awaited as we grow:
Alteration is a part of grace.

Qíblah, when emended, though, would cause
Problems for the sultan Méhmet. He,
Wanting to maintain the sacred laws,
Hagia Sophia found would be
Oriented quite improperly.
How to rectify direction-flaws?

Emperor Justinian was proud
Of the church he'd strongly built. And yet
To the Muslim conquest it had bowed
And become a mosque. Direction set
Facing Mecca would be needed. Fret
Not, O Sultan! Gabriel, allowed

By the Lord to come to Mehmet's aid,
Urged him, "Push against that column." Soul
Eager, Allah-aided, thus he made
All the building rightly move. A hole
In the pillar stayed, but this a role
Sacred for the faithful pious played.

Thumb inserted, turn it clockwise. You
(Old, revered tradition likes to tell)
May attain your dearest wishes, who
Thus perform what one may deem a spell,
Allegory-emblem, shepherd-well
Fountaining a wealth of symbol-clue.

12.
Lyrical Response to a Verse in Sura 2 "The Cow"

148. And each one hath a goal toward which he turneth; so vie with one another in good works. Wheresoever ye may be, Allah will bring you all together....

    Each person has a goal to which he turns,
    So vie with one another in good deeds.
    Unending exploration wisdom earns,
    And yet the unifying Spirit heeds

    A higher love, the deepest of our needs,
    And so will bring you all together, yearns
    To help the mind, centrifugal, that speeds
    In upward, outward spiral, or that burns

    In swift elliptic orbit, heart that reads
    A world-enwhirling sciencecrypture, learns
    Humility through pride yet never spurns
    The glory of the quest, nor yet impedes

    The life, the energetic fire that feeds
    The hope that souls to one another leads.

13.
Lyrical Response to a Verse in Sura 2 "The Cow"

164. Lo! in the creation of the heavens and the earth, and the difference of night and day, and the ships which run upon the sea with that which is of use to men, and the water which Allah sendeth down from the sky, thereby reviving the earth after its death, and dispersing all kinds of beasts therein, and (in) the ordinance of the winds, and the clouds obedient between heaven and earth: are signs (of Allah's sovereignty)....

> In Allah's world to be is to become,
> To breathe, to run, to alter, and to move:
> Who doesn't add, subtracting from the sum
> No ádept in the truth-pursuit will prove.
> When static in your walled-in thinking, you've
> No role in motion's flow-continuum.
>
> The day and night must alternate their rule;
> Upon the sea the useful ship will run:
> The rain-descent revives the world, and you'll
> Inhale the plenitude which had begun
> With wind-creation, heaven-benison,
> When *álif*-breath infused in Adam fuel.
>
> The Lord His creatures widely will disperse
> And make them colorful in sundry kinds;
> The ordinance of winds, the universe
> Enlivening with mindfulness, enwinds
> The breathing of the sky and earth: one finds
> Twin pleasures—to emerge and to immerse.
>
> The welcome by the cloud of mercy-dew
> Up-climbing, coming down again in rain—
> Does fertile work in fostered field made new,
> Filled more with bliss than heart can well contain.
> To change, to die and rise, our wane and gain,
> Our wakefulness and pain, are One-in-two.

14.
Lyrical Response to Verses in Suras 2 "The Cow," 10 "Jonah"

2:256. There is no compulsion in religion. . . .

10:100. And if thy Lord willed, all who are in the earth would have believed together. Wouldst thou (Muhammad) compel men until they are believers? 101. It is not for any soul to believe save by the permission of Allah. . . .

> Whom God has made to differ in belief no man
> May force to utter lies. Conformity against
> The will of conscience? Always wrong. The Lord commenced
> Our being with our freedom. Never tyrant can
>
> Annihilate our best, our Eden-realm of will.
> Let lauded laws of liberty, alert, be tensed
> Protecting freedom, vigil-eye well recompensed
> That heaven-breath may be the health of spirit still.
>
> There's no compulsion in religion. Our respect
> With love concentering, we honor intellect,
> A flowing current, like our circulating blood
>
> Whereof the happily self-regulated flood
> Is purified: in living nature as in art
> Primeval Adam-freedom answers to the heart.

15.
Lyrical Response to a Verse in Sura 2 "The Cow"

256. There is no compulsion in religion. . . .

There's no compulsion in religion. Doubt
Will set us on a path. We're made to move.
How else an untried pow'r of spirit prove?
The rainbow and the peacock-tail spread out

Suggest the one of many made were best.
We're many-minded, -mooded, many-sensed:
Alert, all faculties well tuned and tensed,
We, skeptical, are readied for a test.

There's no compulsion in religion. No
Negation's inadmissible to mind
If I sincerely will a way to find
Enabling me, survival-wise, to grow.

"There is no God—" You stop? Let one whose thought
Had not reached farther honestly then say
What statement he'd arrived at on his way;
"—but Allah" possibly may come unsought.

I learned this from a Sufi who had taught
That should all Truth before us now be laid
At once, all heav'n in blazing heart displayed,
Our journey and our Jordan would be nought.

We creatures are for day and darkness made
And granted gratitude in quiet night,
Her mystery in gleaming stars bedight,
Deep ocean in her whispering embayed.

The angels' nature makes them all obey;
The flaming jinn is tempted to rebel.
We humans, fire-and-mire, cannot compel
Ourselves to find, nor lie should ever say.

There's no compulsion in religion. We
Are favored with a vast poetic gift
Of shaping in similitudes. Uplift
Your face to heav'n, walk tall, think valiantly.

16.
Lyrical Response to Verses in Sura 2 "The Cow"

260. And when Abraham said (unto his Lord): My Lord! Show me how Thou givest life to the dead, He said: Dost thou not believe? Abraham said: Yes, but (I ask) in order that my heart may be at ease. (His Lord) said: Take four of the birds and cause them to incline unto thee, then place a part of them on each hill, then call them, they will come to thee in haste. And know that Allah is Mighty, Wise.

261. The likeness of those who spend their wealth in Allah's way is as the likeness of a grain which groweth seven ears, in every ear a hundred grains. Allah giveth increase manifold to whom He will. Allah is All-Embracing, All-Knowing.

> Iqbal imagined that he heard
> Great Allah to the Prophet say,
> "What fate shall I for you today
> Inscribe?" And so the two conferred.
>
> I think we similarly may
> Interpret the Qur'anic word
> Of Abraham and of the bird
> Assembly in this winning way.
>
> Said Abraham, "Lord, show me how
> You resurrect the dead." "Tame four
> Young doves you place on hills. They'll soar
> In haste, returning." Let's allow
>
> For seeming chance, and hidden law,
> And what we hope, and what we make:
> With Abram's effort—no mistake—
> It was a fate conferred he saw.
>
> The more the earnest work that we
> Invest, fine actions to achieve,
> The likelier, we can believe,
> A pleasant recompense may be.

So they that spend their wealth in ways
Commendable are as the grain
Which manifold re-came, a gain
That freedom-mated fate may raise.

17.
Lyrical Response to Verses in Sura 2 "The Cow"

263. A kind word with forgiveness is better than almsgiving followed by injury. Allah is Absolute, Clement.
264. O ye who believe! Render not vain your almsgiving by reproach and injury, like him who spendeth his wealth only to be seen of men. . . . His likeness is as the likeness of a rock whereon is dust of earth; a rainstorm smiteth it, leaving it smooth and bare. They have no control of aught of that which they have gained. . . .
265. And the likeness of those who spend their wealth in search of Allah's pleasure, and for the strengthening of their souls, is as the likeness of a garden on a height. The rainstorm smiteth it and it bringeth forth its fruit twofold. And if the rainstorm smite it not, then the shower. . . .

> The likeness of a garden on a height,
> The breath of heaven in the freshened air
> Speed up the blood while sharpening the sight,
> Divesting windy spirit of its care.
> The rain is near, a steady aid is there—
> What levity in elevated light!
>
> But one who'd followed alms with bitter spite,
> Ungenerous, luck undisposed to share,
> A lonely, hardened heart—should thunder smite
> That soul, a dusty rock, now bald and bare,
> Behold the ruined waste: of plague beware!
> Forgone is love—and done for, all delight.
>
> With noble faith, no diffidence to blight,
> By storm and shower nourished let us dare
> The morning welcome, and salute the night,
> And field-work beautify in fragrance rare.
> We're grateful in a calm contentment fair:
> The likeness of a garden on a height.

18.
Lyrical Response to Verses in Sura 2 "The Cow"

273. (Alms are) for the poor who are straitened for the cause of Allah, who cannot travel in the land (for trade). The unthinking man accounteth them wealthy because of their restraint. Thou shalt know them by their mark: They do not beg of men with importunity. And whatsoever good thing ye spend, lo! Allah knoweth it.

274. Those who spend their wealth by night and day, by stealth and openly, verily their reward is with their Lord, and there shall no fear come upon them neither shall they grieve.

> The poor whose means are narrowed for the Lord,
> Who cannot travel in the land for trade
> Or pilgrimage—let them receive reward
> From wealthy folk who've more provision made:
> The generous are they who will unlade
> From ample store what they can well afford.
>
> The poor don't beg with importunity
> But rather keep a dignified restraint—
> So have unthinking people failed to see
> Who is in need, and theirs the moral taint
> Of gift-omission while their fellows faint:
> Repentant, work on giving, steadily.
>
> Who gladly spend their wealth by night and day
> Have their reward on high with Him Who'll give—
> The generous their holy Mentor's way
> But follow, He the Sun to all that live:
> Uncovetous and inacquisitive,
> We will from need and grieving sheltered stay.

19.
Lyrical Response to a Verse in Sura 2 "The Cow," Talmud Verse

285. . . . *Unto Thee is the journeying.*
286. *Allah tasketh not a soul beyond its scope. . . . Our Lord! Condemn us not if we forget, or miss the mark! . . . Impose not on us that which we have not the strength to bear! Pardon us, absolve us and have mercy on us, Thou our Protector. . . .*

Chapters of the Fathers *[a Talmudic tractate]* 2:21. *[Rabbi Tarfon] used to say: You are not called upon to complete the work, yet you are not free to evade it. . . .*

> To Life on High continue journeying,
> To Infinite concealed in finite scope.
> To feel the mystery in love and hope
> Can lend to man the speed of spirit-wing.

> If this be doctrine wise, a thing that lies beyond
> Our human strength we'll never be required to bear.
> No honest heart need fear the prospect in his prayer
> Of being overwrought, save by the weighty bond

> Of guilt unpardoned, yet to work and not evade
> The burden of attempting hourly to retry
> A further journeying to meet the Life on High
> Enables me, the rearisen, to unlade

> My care, who must in mental fetter grope.
> The Prophet-sandal touched the heaven-throne:
> O flight of the alone to the Alone!
> May blest Beyondness crown my chronotope.

20.
Lyrical Response to a Verse in Sura 2 "The Cow"

286. Allah tasketh not a soul beyond its scope. . . . Our Lord! Impose not on us that which we have not the strength to bear! Pardon us, absolve us and have mercy on us. . . .

God loads no soul beyond its scope.
Then why the need to utter hope
He won't impose on us what we
Can't bear? 'Mid phantom shadows grope

The seekers, weak, who don't yet see
Past anguishing, that narrowly
Confines the eye, constrained in jail.
We know that feeling: how to free

Despairers from the fear to fail?
The wan entreater, waning, pale,
I glimpse within, beyond would go . . .
Remediator here I hail:

Let pardon, shriving, mercy show
A guardian comfort, so we'll know
In strength an ending of remorse—
My limit-burden I'll outgrow.

Forgiveness will retrieve my force;
Then may renewal take its course:
Poetic sweep of energy—
My blest Buraq, the heaven-horse.

Some feel condemned to self—why be
Unpardoned, unregarded? We
Need not bewildered moan and mope:
Within let spread that Clemency.

21.
Lyrical Response to Verses in Suras 3 "The Family of 'Imrân," 24 "Light"

3:7. . . . . those in whose hearts is doubt pursue, forsooth, that which is allegorical seeking (to cause) dissension by seeking to explain it.

24:35. Allah is the Light of the heavens and the earth. The similitude of His light is as a niche wherein is a lamp. The lamp is in a glass. The glass is as it were a shining star. (This lamp is) kindled from a blessed tree, an olive neither of the East nor of the West, whose oil would almost glow forth (of itself) though no fire touched it. Light upon light. Allah guideth unto His light whom He will. And Allah speaketh to mankind in allegories, for Allah is Knower of all things.

Though some with troubled heart foment
A disputation-filled dissent,
Yet those unfazed, of poet-heart
Adore the allegoric art.

The Knower of all things, our Source
To mortals total Solar force
Cannot unshielded quite convey
Lest eye be blinded by the day.

The oil of truth entire can glow
Before it is enkindled, grow
Yet brighter in the lamplight, star
Become when glassed, though glimpsed afar.

In allegory, likeness-wise,
That ray can travel to the eyes
Of beings finite in their range
Proportioned to a scale of change.

In evanescence metaphor
Is made though veiled, an open door
Wherethrough a higher star unseen
Can light effuse, two realms between.

The dark whereof the light was made
To guide our eyes, encased in shade
Of limit must remain that we
Transpierce, if intermittently.

22.
Lyrical Response to Verses in Suras 3 "The Family of 'Imrân," 62 "The Congregation"

3:7. He it is Who hath revealed unto thee (Muhammad) the Scripture wherein are clear revelations—They are the substance of the Book—and others (which are) allegorical. But those in whose hearts is doubt pursue, forsooth, that which is allegorical seeking (to cause) dissension by seeking to explain it. . . .

62:2. He it is Who hath sent among the unlettered ones a messenger of their own, to recite unto them His revelations and to make them grow, and to teach them the Scripture and Wisdom. . . .

An allegoric page contention makes
If men with quarrel-heart create mistakes:
Interpretation aiding souls to grow
Is morning light outspread on mountain lakes.

Unlettered was the Prophet as we know:
Unfettered on the way that he would go,
Uncluttered open mind would he display;
Unuttered holy teaching would he show.

To learn as when you work or when you pray
With heav'n-receptive heart attention pay
To see the words with bright receiving eye
And hear with ear of welcome what they say.

The brain must offer changeable reply
To altered landscape while we're passing by;
The dawning of creation reawakes
The mind as water lightened by the sky.

23.
Lyrical Response to Verses in Suras 3 "The Family of 'Imrân," 39 "The Troops"

3:84. Say (O Muhammad): We believe in Allah and that which is revealed unto us and that which was revealed unto Abraham and Ishmael and Isaac and Jacob and the tribes, and that which was vouchsafed unto Moses and Jesus and the Prophets from their Lord. We make no distinction between any of them, and unto Him we have surrendered.

39:22. Is he whose bosom Allah hath expanded for the Surrender (unto Him), so that he followeth a light from his Lord (as he who disbelieveth)?

> For loved Surrender unto God, our breast will He
> Expand, we're told within the sura called "The Troops":
> Mind-widened, heart new-freshened, let us join the groups
> That Abraham and sons and grandchild readily
>
> Had led to heaven in that same surrendering
> With Adam, Noah, Enoch, Eber, Sáleh, Lot,
> Job, Jethro, Aaron, Moses, David, rightly thought
> To be a favored one, like Solomon, wise king;
>
> Elijah and Elisha, Joseph, Jonah, too;
> Ezekiel and Zachariah, Baptist John
> And Jesus, and Muhammad—panoramic view
>
> Of Prophets! Make among them no distinction, true
> Proclaimers of the Name, their bodies of the dawn:
> Our daybreak-aiders they, gold flame in molten blue.

24.
Lyrical Response to Verses in Suras 4 "Women," 5 "The Table Spread," 6 "Cattle," 42 "Counsel"

4:40. *Lo! Allah wrongeth not even of the weight of an ant; and if there is a good deed, He will double it and will give (the doer) from His presence an immense reward.*

5:32. *. . . and whoso saveth the life of one, it shall be as if he had saved the life of all mankind.*

6:161. *Whoso bringeth a good deed will receive tenfold the like thereof. . . .*

42:23. *. . . And whoso scoreth a good deed, We add unto its good for him. Lo! Allah is Forgiving, Responsive.*

>When man-surrender to the More-Than-World
>Is undergone, the metaphoric thrust
>Of doubled or of tenfold number must
>Return, so far the height of mind-throw hurled.
>
>The recompense for deed of love our dust
>Will more than humble, as all number pales
>In awe: before the Sun our umber fails,
>Blown upborne motes in livid-thridded gust.
>
>Who saved the life of one, it yet shall be
>As if he'd saved the life of humankind:
>Existence left all finitude behind.
>
>Our life is gift, and infinite; when we
>In heart-requital dart replying ray,
>We, more than whirled, the More-Than-World repay.

25.
Lyrical Response to Verses in Sura 5 "The Table Spread"

44. Lo! We did reveal the Torah, wherein is guidance and a light. . . .

46. We bestowed on [Jesus] the Gospel wherein is guidance and a light. . . .

48. And unto thee [Muhammad] We revealed the Scripture with the truth, confirming whatever Scripture was before it, and a watcher over it. . . . For each [tradition] We have appointed a divine law and a traced-out way. Had Allah willed He could have made you one community. But that He may try you by that which He hath given you (He hath made you as ye are). So vie one with another in good works. . . .

>Our God belauded all the three traditions made.
>There could have been but one community. He might
>Have simplified the tale—the same it would have stayed—
>But better liked the lively change of guiding light.
>
>The variable pageant rainbowed on the white:
>The traveler in realms of likenesses portrayed
>Unloosed a current-flood of wide invention—wade
>Away from shore: extend your metaphoric sight.
>
>The river of the Prophet bore along the bright
>Inheritance of Torah and of Gospel rayed
>In beauty, and he added, loosening the tight
>
>Or narrowing the channel when a depth displayed
>Required a penetration that would love requite
>In water-wandering as wave and breaker swayed.

26.
Lyrical Response to a Verse from Sura 5 "The Table Spread"

110. . . . Allah said: O Jesus, son of Mary! Remember . . . how I taught thee the Scripture and Wisdom and Torah and the Gospel; and how thou didst shape of clay as it were the likeness of a bird by My permission, and didst blow upon it and it was a bird by My permission. . . .

Giotto, a farmer's son, watched the flock of his father and drew pictures of the animals in the sand. It so happened that one day Cimabue accidentally came by, recognized the boy's miraculous talent, and took the boy with him. Under his guidance, Giotto grew up to be the great genius of the new Italian art.
. . . The tale of Christ as a young sculptor of animals was undoubtedly familiar to those Florentines who "invented" the legend of the discovery of talent. (Ernst Kris, Psychoanalytic Explorations in Art *[New York: Schocken, 1952], 68, 70)*

Here's a rhythm guide to the stanza form. A slash means a strong syllable and an x a weak one.

/x /x x/ /x x/ x/
/x /x x/ /x x/ x/
   /x /x x/x
 /x /x x/ x/

      Cattle seen in the sand, bird in the reddened clay,
      Adam glimpsed in the ground, fruit of the garden soil,
         God and sculptor together
      Frame the dream of emergent youth.

      Scripture, wisdom, and art: Gospel and Torah, too,
      Join Qur'an to presént hope of a poet-craft,
         Bird calligraphy winging,
      Footprint-mark on the skein of sky.

Soul, when viewing the birds over the mead, will think
Back to Crete when the scribe followed the plowman's path,
  Rightward writing, then leftward,
    Flight of mind on the furrows drawn.

Jesus, Giotto, and me: Spirit, you aid us all;
Hand—a statue itself, telling the mind to shape
  Names for animal, angel,
    Tribe and kind of the creature world.

27.
Lyrical Response to Verses in Sura 5 "The Table Spread"

110. . . . Allah said: O Jesus, son of Mary! Remember My favour unto thee and unto thy mother; how I strengthened thee with the holy Spirit, so that thou spakest unto mankind in the cradle as in maturity; and how I taught thee the Scripture and Wisdom and the Torah and Gospel; and how thou didst shape of clay as it were the likeness of a bird by My permission, and didst blow upon it and it was a bird by My permission, and thou didst heal him who was born blind and the leper by My permission; and how didst raise the dead, by My permission. . . .

Yes, Allah Scripture, Wisdom, Torah, Gospel taught
To Jesus; holy Spirit aiding, in him wrought
The pow'r to teach, when yet he in the cradle lay,
The willing pilgrim who embodied doctrine sought.

By God's permission Jesus made a bird of clay
And breathing on it sent it flying on its way;
He was allowed to raise the dead, make see the blind
And heal the leper—glory-deed of storied sway.

The Scripture, Wisdom, Torah, Gospel humankind
From Jesus learned. Muhammad's followers will find—
So God would underline in telling of it here—
Three Abrahamic legacies are intertwined.

The Jesus-bird through heaven flying will appear
To them who resurrected feel, each day and year:
"Light spirit-being granted never can be caught
Or caged!" proclaims the heart unaging, free of fear.

28.
Lyrical Response to a Verse in Sura 6 "Cattle"

25. Of these [hearers] are some who listen unto thee [Muhammad], but We have placed upon their hearts veils, lest they should understand, and in their ears a deafness. If they saw every token they would not believe therein. . . .

    The revelation penetrating, great the calm
    That will pervade and overspread your central being—
    For what you gain is to attain a way of seeing
    Engendering your all from the almighty AUM.

    You speak, and maybe find your hearer disagreeing
    That value may be found in light-expanding dawn,
    In rushing wind of spirit? Love will carry on.
    We reach the core of comprehension, guaranteeing

    A cleansing mental healing when we realize
    The seeming veilings that the ireful might despise
    Have often come from trying losses that arise
    From dire affliction yet portrayed in weeping eyes.

    The people you will meet had variedly been schooled,
    With spirit-freedom that can not be overruled.
    The will of Allah, giving liberty its weight,
    Is bodied forth when will and limit generate

    A history where sight and blindness interblend,
    Nor ever will the dappled pattern have an end
    So long as time remain the paper where we draw
    The struggle of the dark with holy heart of awe—

    So long as change may ask that we on canvas paint
    An epic of the bold and weak, the brave and faint—
    So long as life may be the scroll whereon we write
    The combat of our fear with comrade-loving light.

29.
Lyrical Response to a Verse in Sura 6 "Cattle"

38. There is not an animal in the earth, nor a flying creature flying on two wings, but they are peoples like unto you. We have neglected nothing in the Book [of Our decrees]. . . .

There is no animal nor flying thing,
But they are tribes and peoples like to you:
So in the book of nature's world-decrees
The thought is written that we ought to hear.

We understand: the deer are threatening
Our many kinds of plants; and not a few
Have died, through grazing, of our youthful trees;
And soon may varied species disappear.

But: kill nine-tenths of blameless grazers? Fling
Them on a huge cadaver-pile, bestrew
The field with butchery? They'd bring disease,
We're told, if they were moved, and rangers fear

They'd die, in competition, by the spring
Wherever they were brought. So what to do?
They overreproduce? Yet feeling sees
The carnage, and a grief the heart will sear.

I am no guide; I have no secret ring
To rub and solve the problem. If we slew
The deer, however, evil memories
Would visit us with nightmares bleak and blear.

Whatever else may happen, mind may spring
To action, frame a well-considered view
Of how to serve Creation best. And, please!
Plan in advance to rescue what is dear!

30.
Lyrical Response to a Verse in Sura 6 "Cattle"

159. Wait they, indeed, for nothing less than that the angels should come unto them, or thy Lord should come, or there should come one of the portents from thy Lord? In the day when one of the portents from thy Lord cometh, its belief availeth naught a soul which theretofore believed not, nor in its belief earned good (by works). Say: Wait ye! Lo! We (too) are waiting.

Im Gewahrwerden der Schönheit der Welt und ihrer Wunder werden uns auch die Bürden des Daseins leichter. Man muß nur Augen, Ohren und alle Sinne auftun, dann wird selbst einem schwer Beladenen wohler zumute. [In becoming aware of the beauty of the world and of its wonders we find also the burdens of existence becoming lighter. One need only open eyes, ears, and all the senses in order for even a person heavy laden to feel heartened.]—Letter from Katharina Mommsen

> In scanning omens from the Lord they prove their skill
> In whom an avid plant and swoop of wing instill
> A portrait and a portent, swift unbidden glint
> In cryptic wind, of heart-spark, of a hidden will.
>
> An omen to a stone means little. *Let there be
> A light* implied *Let there be eyes alive to see:*
> A *rosa mundi*, seven-rayed, conveys a hint
> Of unexampled candelabral majesty.
>
> An ear, an eye, a mouth, a nose—each opening
> A window or a door, no force or active thing,
> Until the dweller in the body-home arise
> To be the owner of that castle, and its king.
>
> The master of the temple-mansion can awake
> Through empathy that will perception lend and take:
> Unburden bird, begem the grass, ignite the skies,
> The shadow draw that waking branch at dawn shall make.

31.
Lyrical Response to a Verse in Sura 7 "The Heights"

57. And He it is Who sendeth the winds as tidings heralding His mercy, till, when they bear a cloud heavy (with rain), We lead it to a dead land, and then cause water to descend thereon and thereby bring forth fruits of every kind. Thus bring We forth the dead. . . .

    And He it is who sendeth winds, their tidings heralding
    His mercy till they bear a heavy cloud replete with rain.
    We lead it to a deadland, causing water to descend,
    So nourishing and fostering the fruits of every kind.
            Thus bring we forth the dead.

    The cloud is like a river that its water glad would fling
    In foam abroad, above, across the rocks: the ocean main
    Will so be frenzied, tide-borne triumph bearing, to befriend
    The shore with gem of shell and statue-driftwood lads will find
            By hope of treasure led.

    The poet pondering the things to come for theme to sing
    Is going to consider youth a dream for man-refrain
    Recurrently to sound as a remembrance: he the end
    Of Being so can link with his beginning, letting mind
            To sea and cloud be wed.

32.
Lyrical Response to Verses in Suras 7 "The Heights," 25 "The Criterion"

7:57. And He it is Who sendeth the winds as tidings heralding His mercy, till, when they bear a cloud heavy (with rain), We lead it to a dead land, and then cause water to descend thereon and thereby bring forth fruits of every kind. Thus bring We forth the dead. . . .

25:47. And He it is Who maketh night a covering for you, and sleep repose, and maketh day a resurrection.

    And He it is Who made the day a resurrection,
        And with a storm brings forth the dead.
      For Gabriel by heaven-strength is led
    Not with a trumpet call to summon to inspection

      The grave-awakened soul—flute-music-fed
    Are we who join prophetic birds to foil dejection,
    Who joy, alert, to hear the clever tune-selection
        Whereby the sky and soil are wed.

Behold the worlds arise, of one accord in glory
Agleam in prostrate glisten-grasses, and with eye
    Asparkle in our hearkening, who sigh:
      The myrrh of that eternal story,

As of the fragrance in the garment-allegory,
    Aroma that by Joseph-guidance high
A sight revived would grant, to me today brought nigh
      The Jacob-moment of satori.

33.
Lyrical Response to Verses in Suras 7 "The Heights," 59 "Exile," 73 "The Enshrouded One"

7:143. And when his Lord revealed (His) glory to the mountain He sent it crashing down. And Moses fell down senseless. And when he woke he said: Glory unto Thee! I turn unto Thee repentant, and I am the first of (true) believers.

59:21. If We had caused this Qur'ân to descend upon a mountain, thou (O Muhammad) verily hadst seen it humbled, rent asunder by the fear of Allah. Such similitudes coin We for mankind, that haply they may reflect.

73:5. For we shall charge thee with a word of weight.
6. Lo! the vigil of the night is (a time) when impression is more keen and speech more certain.

> The Allah-glory sent the mountain crashing down
> And first in true-believing made of Moses then.
> The strength of the similitudes God framed for men
> Will humble, yet present the mind a shining crown.
>
> The poet, as a shaper of similitudes,
> A thought of higher grace will bear in word of weight—
> The import grave, yet will the light of heav'n elate,
> For solemn joy is the supreme of human moods.
>
> In vigil of the night, impression is more keen
> A metaphor to grasp, and chanting speech more certain,
> The tranquil, ample, still surrender more serene.
>
> The veil is lifted, and we're led, beyond the curtain,
> Past allegory, parable of deeper things,
> To Him, the symbols' symbol, and the King of Kings.

34.
Lyrical Response to Verses in Suras 7 "The Heights," 12 "Joseph," 21 "The Prophets," 23 "The Believers"

7:150. And when Moses returned unto his people, angry and grieved, he said, Evil is that (course) which ye took after I had left you. . . .
151. He said, My Lord! Have mercy on me and on my brother; bring us into thy mercy, Thou the Most Merciful of those who show mercy.

12:90. They said: Is it indeed thou who art Joseph? He said: I am Joseph. . . . Allah hath shown us favour. Lo! he who wardeth off (evil) and endureth (findeth favour): for verily Allah loseth not the wages of the kindly. . . .
92. He said: Have no fear this day! May Allah forgive you, and He is the Most Merciful of those who show mercy.

21:83. And Job . . . cried unto his Lord, (saying): Lo! adversity afflicted me, and Thou art Most merciful of all who show mercy.

23:118. And (O Muhammad) say: My Lord! Forgive and have mercy, for Thou art best of all who show mercy.

> *You are the best of all who mercy show.*
> By this will we the true preferment know:
> You Moses' anger at the golden calf
> Had cooled, and let the stream of pardon flow.
>
> *You are the best of all who mercy show.*
> When brothers treated Joseph as a foe,
> He winnowed out the feelings' wheat from chaff
> And, God-taught, loving token would bestow.
>
> *You are the best of all who mercy show.*
> When Job had sensed a hot resentment glow
> While Iblis mocked him with demonic laugh,
> He, yielding not, in heartfelt strength would grow.
>
> *You are the best of all who mercy show.*
> How well the Prophet knew it! For although
> Qur'an appeared obscure as cryptograph,
> He'd, reading it, an angel-aiding know.

35.
Lyrical Response to Verses in Sura 7 "The Heights"

156. . . . My mercy embraceth all things, therefore I shall ordain it for those who ward off (evil) and pay the poor-due, and those who believe Our revelations;
157. Those who follow the messenger, the Prophet who can neither read nor write, whom they will find described in the Torah and the Gospel (which are) with them.

Everything My mercy can embrace:
Therefore I'm ordaining it for those
Who, averting evil with their grace,
Feel what earth awaked from winter knows:
Lord is loaf-ward; nightingale and rose
Open odic and aroma space.

Those who hearken to Our messenger,
Prophet who can neither read nor write,
Speaking what the Torah will aver,
Saying what the Gospel bathed in light,
In Our robes of mercy are bedight:
Heard from Gabriel, the word of myrrh.

Pay the poor-due, give to all who need
Care like what the Prophet had received:
Had a noble soul not paid him heed
Who was early orphaned, greatly grieved,
Think today how we would feel bereaved:
Free the flame. And scatter light-ray seed.

36.
Lyrical Response to a Verse in Sura 9 "Repentance"

12. Fain would they put out the light of Allah with their mouths, but Allah disdaineth (aught) save that He shall perfect His light, however much the disbelievers are averse.

. . . God will perfect His Light, i.e., make it shine all the brighter in the eyes of men. His Light in itself is ever perfect, but it will penetrate the hearts of men more and more, and so become more and more perfect for them. (A. Yusuf Ali, trans., The Holy Qur'ān 449 n1289.)

>The mind of God we cannot know
>Except through lordly metaphor
>And so were made that we might grow
>And make, for mind, that Light the more.
>
>Analogy, in ample speech—
>Heart's art-will in the world you see—
>A whisper, ev'n, may gladly teach
>Lamp's gleaming actuality.
>
>In parable of deed and word,
>By act of utterance and toil,
>We've candle-wick for image-oil:
>
>If God the Sun-Creator be,
>We echo thus the tone that He
>Made seen when *Let it be* was heard.

37.
Lyrical Response to Verses in Sura 9 "Repentance"

9:26. Then Allah sent His peace of reassurance down upon His messenger and upon the believers, and sent down hosts ye could not see. . . .

40. If ye help him [Muhammad] not, still Allah helped him when those who disbelieve drove him forth, the second of two: when they two were in the cave, when he said unto his comrade: Grieve not. Lo! Allah is with us. Then Allah caused His peace of reassurance to descend upon him and supported him with hosts ye cannot see. . . .

How manifold the Peace of Reassurance we
Upon the bondsmen of the One descending see:
Thus Abu Bakr would the Prophet in the cave
With tranquil aiding grace the Heaven's Helper save.

The persecuting foes benignly were deceived
By Him that helped the faithful hearers who believed:
A tree the Lord made rise, to hide the opening;
The web a spider wove would more concealment bring.

A dove then laid her egg to block the entrance way
And make it seem as if no folk had come to stay.
The patient comrade, dying, bitten by a snake,
Lay silent: he declined the Holy Man to wake.

But Peace of Reassurance Allah would provide,
Made doubly strong where brother-friendship will abide.
The Prophet, God-bestirred, saliva-cure applied
And healed the wound with holy strength, and no one died.

38.
Lyrical Response to Verses in Sura 10 "Jonah"

12. If Allah were to hasten on for men the ill (that they have earned) as they would hasten on the good, their respite would already have expired. But We suffer those who look not for the meeting with Us to wander blindly on in their contumacy.

13. And if misfortune touch a man he crieth unto Us, (while reclining) on his side, or sitting or standing, but when We have relieved him of the misfortune he goeth his way as though he had not cried. . . .

20. Mankind were but one community; then they differed; and had it not been for a word that had already gone forth from thy Lord it had been judged between them in respect of that wherein they differ.

> If Allah were to hasten on for men the ill
> That they have earned, as they would hasten on the good,
> Their réspite would have been already ended. Should
> They, blind, in cóntumacy wander, We are still.
>
> And if misfortune touch a man he cries to Us,
> While sitting, standing, or reclining on his side,
> But when it is relieved, as if he hadn't cried,
> "What gratitude?" he'll ask; "there's nothing to discuss."
>
> Men first were one, but later differed in their speech,
> And had a word by God not hitherto been sent,
> They'd no delay have known but felt the judgment lent
> Because intents had varied in the things they teach.
>
> But time is granted by the great Eternity
> That we may live and widen heart and heighten mind:
> A helpful mentor, when you Memory unbind,
> The past will teach the present. Eyes, combining, see.

39.
Lyrical Response to Verses in Suras 10 "Jonah," 14 "Abraham," 36 "Yâ Sîn"

10:10. Lo! those who believe and do good works, their Lord guideth them by their faith. Rivers will flow beneath them in the Gardens of Delight,
11. Their prayer therein will be: Glory be to Thee, O Allah! and their greeting therein will be: Peace. . . .

14:23. And those who believed and did good works are made to enter Gardens underneath which rivers flow, therein abiding by permission of their Lord, their greeting therein: Peace!

36:54. Lo! those who merit paradise this day are happily employed, . . .
56. Theirs the fruit (of their good deeds) and theirs (all) that they ask;
57. The word from a Merciful Lord (for them) is: Peace!

> A triple sura-teaching lent, that war may cease:
> The greeting of these Eden-dwellers, threefold peace.
> Let's heed it, lest the planet perish. Mildly say:
> Down by the riverside our sword and shield we lay.
>
> In life, the only wealth! As river-stream, our breath
> Let flow in tranquil greeting—so the sura saith.
> A garden grown for life and health by knowing heart
> Will charm the Sheba-Queen of Peace with lover-dart.
>
> Yet fruit that valiant deeds may cause to bloom will not
> Fruition reach but blighted be through havoc wrought
> So long as fatal riches made of tainted cash
>
> In weaponry invested turn the grass to ash.
> Reverse the rule of Cain! and may the seed of Seth
> Learn peace, and overturn this brain-invading death.

40.
Lyrical Response to Verses in Sura 10 "Jonah"

16. And when Our clear revelations are recited unto them, they who look not for the meeting with Us say: Bring a Lecture other than this, or change it. Say (O Muhammad): It is not for me to change it of my own accord. I only follow that which is inspired in me. . . .

17. Say: If Allah had so willed I should not have recited it to you nor would He have made it known to you. I dwelt among you a whole lifetime before it (came to me). . . .

> One cannot say when it will come, but when it comes
> I am the instrument whereon the Spirit strums;
> I am the tabret and the flute and barbiton
> The Great Musician's moved to play, then wander on.
>
> The age I have attained will need the tune He makes
> To be entrusted well: I pray that no mistakes
> Appear in my transmittal of the hymn inspired,
> For love-requital means a faithful skill required.
>
> I am the tambourine, the zither, and the drums,
> The chancy mote that to the dancing note succumbs.
> Muhammad forty years had reached at Ramadan
> When revelation came a-borning in Qur'an;
>
> At sixty-one I learned to write the verse that wakes
> When, heard, the surging stir my Adam-hand that shakes:
> A scryer and a scribe may winter singer be
> When cedar bough will sound as if a whirling sea.

41.
Lyrical Response to a Verse in Sura 10 "Jonah"

48. And for every nation there is a messenger. And when their messenger cometh (on the Day of Judgement) it will be judged between them fairly, and they will not be wronged.

For every nation there's a messenger, and on
The Day of Judgment when their messenger will come,
It will be judged between them fairly: they will not
Be wronged. In patience wait for meaning to unfold.

At varied places on the globe the time of dawn
Will vary, and the one we see won't be the sum,
Nor hue the same as for another may be wrought:
Let morning star enskyed be changingly ensouled.

A Christian, Muslim, or an Ophite Gnostic who
The snake exalted, Zoroastrian that fire
In heaven will enkindle, making Rumi, too,

Adore the world-creating strength of sky-desire,
The dervish and the priest, the Buddhist and the Jew,
Their messengers let meet, each other to inspire.

42.
Lyrical Response to Verses in Suras 12 "Joseph," 53 "The Star"

12:30. And women in the city said: The ruler's wife is asking of her slave-boy an ill deed. Indeed he has smitten her to the heart with love. We behold her in plain aberration.

31. And when she heard of their sly talk, she sent to them and prepared for them a cushioned couch (to lie on at the feast) and gave to every one of them a knife and said (to Joseph): Come out unto them! And when they saw him they exalted him and cut their hands, exclaiming: Allah Blameless! This is not a human being. This is no other than some gracious angel.

32. She said: this is he on whose account ye blamed me. I asked of him an evil act, but he proved continent, but if he do not my behest he verily shall be imprisoned, and verily shall be of those brought low.

33. He said: O my Lord! Prison is more dear than that unto which they urge me, and if Thou fend not off their wiles from me I shall incline unto them and become of the foolish.

53:43. And He it is Who maketh laugh, and maketh weep. . . .

> At stories lent us by the heavens' Lord I weep
> Or smile, or both, as He may will. So here I keep
> The laughter and the sadness balanced in the mind:
> Through comedy and sorrow, we reward can reap.
>
> Of Joseph (Yusuf) we the would-be temptress find
> Attempting to explain how lust had made her blind.
> The wife of Potiphar (Aziz we call him here;
> And her, Zuleika) was in love, but wasn't kind.
>
> Now when she calls for Joseph, quickly he'll appear:
> The handsomest in all the land! So diamond-clear
> It is to every flustered lady luncheon-guest,
> They fumble with their fruit-knives, cut their hands—oh dear!
>
> A culprit? No, indeed—a gracious angel blest!
> And, as angelic, ethical—he'd passed the test

Impeccably. He's praying to return to jail
If that's the only way the man may get some rest.

His prayer answered, never sin can him assail:
To God he's grateful, though emaciated, pale.
Adore the Lord alone, Who'll slumber not nor sleep;
Be watchful, lest the lock should break, and patience fail.

43.
Lyrical Response to Suras 12 "Joseph," 79 "'Those Who Drag Forth'"

12:51. He (the king) (then sent for those women and) said: What happened when ye asked an evil act of Joseph? They answered: Allah Blameless! We know no evil of him. Said the wife of the ruler: Now the truth is out. I asked of him an evil act, and he is surely of the truthful.

52. (Then Joseph said: I asked for) this, that he (my lord) may know that I betrayed him not in secret, and that surely Allah guideth not the snare of the betrayers.

53. I do not exculpate myself. Lo! the (human) soul [nafs] enjoineth unto evil, save that whereon my Lord hath mercy. Lo! my Lord is Forgiving, Merciful.

54. And the king said: bring him unto me that I may attach him to my person. And when he had talked with him he said: Lo! thou art to-day in our presence established and trusted.

79:40. But as for him who feared to stand before his Lord and restrained his soul [nafs] from lust,
41. Lo! the Garden will be his home.

> The lower soul enjoins to evil, save when He
> May turn that might aside, the higher soul to free.
> Zuleika served the lower; Joseph paid no heed:
> The day is breaking in his mind: awake and see!
>
> A morning star arising, like a light-borne seed,
> Transformed Zuleika, too, in truth! We hear her plead
> For pardon, though of this the poets only tell.
> The blest Qur'an kept silent: Jami I will read,
>
> For he and other bards a heart-uplifting spell
> Have worked. We learn: Zuleika waited, biding well
> Her time to purify her thought until the day
> She might in higher, soul-devoted love excel.
>
> She waited, and she prayed. Occasion came. A ray
> Illumined Joseph when her husband passed away:

They soon were wed. Aziz, claim some, was impotent
Those many years, that she a virgin yet might stay.

Zuleika and her Joseph both will be content,
For each may illustrate the radiant lesson lent:
Restrain the lower soul, and you will holy be:
Perform the moral norm the Lord for mortals meant.

44.
Lyrical Response to Suras 12 "Joseph," 23 "The Believers"

12:93. Go [O brothers] with this shirt of mine and lay it on my father's face, he will become (again) a seer; and come to me with all your folk.
94. When the caravan departed their father [blind Jacob] had said: Truly I am conscious of the breath of Joseph, though ye call me dotard.
95. (Those around him) said: by Allah, lo! thou art in thine old aberration.
96. Then, when the bearer of glad tidings came, he laid it on his face and he became a seer once more. He said: Said I not unto you that I know from Allah that which ye know not?

23:96. Repel evil with that which is better. . . .

> We've seen the brothers putting Joseph in a pit,
> And there he could have died, had not a caravan
> Come by and sent their water-drawer who, surprised,
> Requested comrades' aid. They saved him, and would sell
>
> Their prize to Potiphar in Egypt. Then a fit
> Of lust attacked the latter's wife. Beleaguered man,
> Yet Joseph, handsomest in all the land, advised
> By Allah, could withstand her wily tempter-spell.
>
> The demon, though, who drove the woman wouldn't quit:
> She's running after Joseph in the hope she can
> Exact what he withheld. Yet she'll have realized
> Her error when her woe to Potiphar she'll tell:
>
> "The culprit merits prison or a painful doom!"
> But Joseph: "*She* it was who asked an evil deed
> Of *me.*" The shirt he wore, the victim had observed,
> Was torn behind: she'd been the hunter, he the prey!
>
> A vindication of our hero: from the room
> In jail he, strength attaining, rose by paying heed
> To God, from Whose commandment never had he swerved.
> And when a famine came, a savior-role he'd play.

His brothers, who would know him, next arrived in gloom,
Requesting bread. And Joseph gladly now will feed
The men (for strong is he in spirit, not unnerved).
What's more, he, holding up the rescue-shirt, can say,

"Our father had been blinded, mourning for his son.
If, on those whitened eyes, the garment you will lay,
Clear vision he'll regain. Indeed he can foresee
The coming wonder now already—go, be blest."

A vindication of the father! Quick—they run
To share the news, to give the food—and sunlit day
To Jacob they'll restore! The shirt has worked, and we
Behold his brightened, loving gaze, the holiest.

Repel the bad with what is better. Once begun,
Forgiveness that originates in Allah may
Irradiate the world as Joseph Egypt. He
A healing pardon spread, an Eden-garden fest.

45
Lyrical Response to Verses in Suras 12 "Joseph," 75 "The Raising of the Dead," 89 "The Dawn"

12:53. I do not exculpate myself. Lo! the (human) soul [nafs] enjoineth unto evil, save that whereon my Lord hath mercy. . . .

75:2. Nay, I swear by the accusing soul [nafs] (that this Scripture is true).

89:27. But ah! thou soul [nafs] at peace!
28. Return unto thy Lord, content in His good pleasure!

. . . Zulaikha (Suleika). . . , the wife of Potiphar, . . . concentrated all her efforts on seducing Joseph (Yusuf). Countless poets have turned to her as a nafs *symbol[;] . . . this* nafs *is purified by boundless love and its resultant fathomless sorrow and is finally united with Yusuf.* (Annemarie Schimmel, My Soul is a Woman, *22 and see 20*)

. . . [B]eautiful is the famous tale in which Dhu 'n-Nun asks an unnamed old woman: "'What is the end of love?' She responded: 'Love has no end.' And I asked: 'Why?' She answered: 'You idiot! Because the Beloved has no end.'" (Schimmel, 82)

> Seducing, then accusing, finally at peace,
> You are Zuleika, O my soul! I feel release
> In union with my heaven-Yusuf, ever blest;
> May each the other's raiment-radiance increase.

> Like Father Jacob, you indeed, as lover-test,
> Were blinded in your grief, yet faith was proven blest;
> My Yusuf-view at length the wonder would repeat
> Whereby the garment pure a blindness had redressed.

> For impotent was poor Aziz: he knew defeat . . .
> But love for you in dream remained for me the sweet
> Envisioned meaning of my trial, woe, travail,
> That chaste and patient I your longed-for gaze might greet.

I trusted that my love a triumph would entail:
It couldn't end, for the Beloved Whom I hail,
For Whom I suffered pain that never seemed to cease,
You bodied forth—your eyes alight behind the veil.

46.
Lyrical Response to Verses in Sura 15 "Al-Ḥijr"

51. And tell them [the servants of Allah] of Abraham's guests,
52. (How) when they came in unto him, and said: Peace. He said: Lo! we are afraid of you.
53. They said: Be not afraid! Lo! we bring thee good tidings of a boy possessing wisdom.
54. He said: Bring ye me good tidings (of a son) when old age hath overtaken me? Of what then can ye bring good tidings?
55. They said: We bring thee good tidings in truth. So be not thou of the despairing.
56. He said: And who despaireth of the mercy of his Lord save those who are astray?

>Our guests unknown we'll seek to greet, not fear.
>And in improbabilities we may
>Consider something hidden that is dear
>And ought not be evaded, waved away:
>A lifetime's coronating glory-day
>Might lie before you in your final year.
>
>The child that came to Abram in his age
>He'd hoped for long, and never had despaired;
>His faith in what an angel might presage
>No weary unbeliever would have dared.
>Unheeding fearers, though, had farther fared
>Had they but reasoned: goals are hopers' wage.
>
>Despair itself is hell; no greater pain
>Can be imposed upon the heart of one
>Who in the daybreak might no faith sustain
>Nor, blinded, can foresee the morning sun.
>Yet much has been determined, dared, and done
>By sufferers and grievers, to their gain.
>
>So Blake had claimed: if sun and moon should doubt
>(As humans wanting will are wont to do)

We'd see that they'd immediately go out.
The night would rule at last, the blackened hue
No shine would more allow. To life then do
As you'd be done by. Sons of heaven, shout!

For who despaireth of the mercy of
The Lord save those that have been led astray?
Surrender but to Him Who throned above
All care must dwell which mortals can affray:
If not in one, then in another way
Be elevated by the leaven, Love.

47.
Lyrical Response to Verses in Sura 15 "Al-Ḥijr"

85. We created not the heavens and the earth and all that is between them save with truth, and lo! the Hour is surely coming. So forgive, O Muhammad, with a gracious forgiveness. . . .
87. We have given thee seven of the oft-repeated (verses) and the great Qurân.
88. Strain not thine eyes toward that which We cause some wedded pairs among them to enjoy, and be not grieved on their account, and lower thy wing (in tenderness) for the believers. . . .
97. Well know We that thy bosom is at times oppressed by what they [the doubters] say,
98. But hymn the praise of thy Lord, and be of those who make prostration (unto Him).
99. And serve the Lord till the inevitable cometh unto thee.

>Be not distraught, but let a feeling of the kind
>To favor wedded love expel a thought forlorn:
>Rejoice in others—let your wing, like dew at morn,
>Be lowered tenderly, with empathy in mind.
>
>What isn't given yet in later time is born;
>If nothing has availed to wake the spirit-blind,
>The wealth enduring in prophetic word you find
>Will shame the vanity of envy and of scorn.
>
>The bird that young ones can with shelter of her wing
>Protect from predator and from the winds that fling
>The peril of their chill in frenzied winter whirr
>
>Be emblem of your care as our remembrancer:
>So make prostration, sing a hymn, and woe eloign,
>Then, humble, serve. He comes—Whom you in joy will join.

48.
Lyrical Response to Verses in Sura 16 "The Bee"

15. And He hath cast into the earth firm hills that it quake not with you, and streams and roads that ye may find a way.
16. And landmarks (too), and by the star they find a way.

36. And verily We have raised in every nation a messenger, (proclaiming): Serve Allah and shun false gods. Then some of them (there were) whom Allah guided, and some of them (there were) upon whom error had just hold. Do but travel in the land and see the nature of the consequence for the deniers!

    The guides without us are abundant, that we be
    Secured, confirmed by stream and star, and hill and tree;
    And every tribe and nation gains a messenger
    That in its tongue will render what the worlds prefer.

    Upon what kind of man has error taken hold?
    Go travel in the land, and see the nature of
    The consequence for the deniers of that love
    Bespoken all about us by the manifold.

    We are ungrounded, never steady as the hills;
    We fail to ward the river: water overspills
    A barren shore made naked of a leafy shade.

    Then gaze before you now: the chaos we have made
    Grows daily—waken, fainting mind, look near and far!
    Our land has mirrored the deniers that we are.

49.
Lyrical Response to Verses in Sura 16 "The Bee"

48. Have they not observed all things that Allah hath created, how their shadows incline on the right and to the left, making prostration unto Allah, and they are lowly?

49. And unto Allah maketh prostration whatsoever is in the heavens and whatsoever is in the earth of living creatures, and the angels (also), and they are not proud.

The "shadows" suggest how all things in this life are mere shadows of the true Reality in heaven; and they should turn and move in accordance with the divine light, as the shadows of trees and buildings move in one direction or another, and lengthen or shorten according to the light from heaven. (A. Yusuf Ali, trans., The Holy Qur'ān, 668 n. 2074)

>A part, or version, or a representative
>Or emblem of a tree or building, people too,
>Will move and make prostration as the changing view
>The altered light will shed that made us be and live.
>
>The forms of gray on ground a mirror-picture give
>As creature-colors will reveal the light wherethrough
>The iris, eye and rainbow, each diverse of hue,
>Will feel the universal, perfect, purposive.
>
>Essential flame of jinn—will this a shadow cast?
>Or will an angel? Of them both, reflection passed
>From up above, and lay upon me, stroked my soul.
>
>Though immaterial the higher mirroring,
>It was a dart to stimulate my heart to sing:
>Reflecting, I reply. That art will make me whole.

50.
Lyrical Response to Verses in Sura 16 "The Bee"

48. *Have they not observed all things that Allah hath created, how their shadows incline to the right and to the left, making prostration unto Allah, and they are lowly?*

68. *And thy Lord inspired the bee, saying: Choose thou habitations in the hills and in the trees and in that which they thatch:*
69. *Then eat of all fruits, and follow the ways of thy Lord, made smooth (for thee). There cometh forth from their bellies a drink diverse of hues, wherein is healing for mankind. Lo! herein is indeed a portent for people who reflect.*

> The shadows cast of rambling animals and plants
> Are like the honey, many-hued, of agile bees:
> Reflection may we see in those, and so in these,
> Of One made plural-viewed, our wonder to advance.
>
> The creatures on the thatch of roofs and in the trees
> Or hovering above a hill our life enhance
> With sweet of yellow, brown, and tan, and white: in dance
> What they have drunken sung may bloom and human please.
>
> The shadows, the reflections, and the colors all
> Let's never then transcend entirely! For we fall
> To unperceiving apathy when we forget
>
> The glimpse of Infinite that by the Manifold
> Our questing minds in the direction have been set
> Which leads to One beyond what creature can behold.

51.
Lyrical Response to Verses in Sura 16 "The Bee"

68. And thy Lord inspired the bee, saying: Choose thou habitations in the hills and in the trees and in that which they thatch;
69. Then eat of all fruits, and follow the ways of thy Lord, made smooth (for thee). There cometh forth from their bellies a drink diverse of hues, wherein is healing for mankind. Lo! herein is indeed a portent for people who reflect.

Jauchzend umarmten Dich da die Weiber der Korübanten,
Sie die Nümphen des Dikte; und in goldener Wiege
Liess Adrasteia Dich ruhn; die süsse Milch Amaltheiens
War Dein Trank und Deine Speise lieblicher Honig.
Ihn bereiteten Dir die Panakrischen emsigen Bienen
Auf dem hohen waldumschatteten Gipfel Panakrons.

—Kallimachos, "Zeushymnus," trans. Wilhelm von Humboldt, Griechische Gedichte, *ed. Horst Rüdiger, Ernst Heimeran Press, Munich, 3rd ed. 1936*

Joyful the women embraced you, the corybants, avid bacchantes,
Nymphs of fair Dicte, and then in your beautiful gold-fashioned cradle
Set you to rest Adrasteia; sweet milk Amaltheia provided
Glad would you drink, and your food was the ever most lovely, the honey—
This the Panácrean bees, the industrious, quickly preparing
High on Panácron, the summit by shading arboreal covered.

See how the Greek had predicted the Prophet: the trees will be planted,
Nourishing those who will honey distill, of a savor delightful,
Right for the bravest of rulers. For so did the Lord of the Daybreak
Fitly decree when the Sun of His Being illumined Creation.
Honey and milk are the food of the poet who, mind ever active,
Present and lesson from Nature with ardor ingesting, imbibing,
Wisely inventive, awake, will a morning-transformative lyric
Shape to convey what a dream had revealed to him lately of wonder.

52.
Lyrical Response to Verses in Suras 16 "The Bee," 17 "The Children of Israel"

16:125. Call unto the way of thy Lord with wisdom and fair exhortation, and reason with them in the better way. . . .
126. . . . if ye remain patient, verily it is better for the patient.
17:11. Man prayeth for evil as he prayeth for good; for man was ever hasty.

    It may be true for man, I'm sure it is for me,
    Who pray for what I think is good too hastily:
    To reason circumspectly in the better way
    Will calm the eye for wisdom, help the psalmer see.

    The agent who's impatient can be led astray:
    He doesn't act but suffers, dwelling on the day
    Of sated want, to speed his evening, thus to be
    Forgetful of what morn before him will display.

    As meditator it is better far to pray
    Than suppliant, whom underlying doubts affray:
    Of *pray* the cognate verb is *fragen, ask*. And we
    Are well advised: inquire within for spirit-ray.

    An hourly useful tool is etymology,
    And what is fate but something *fatum, said?* The free
    Will seek Recital Night, that secret teaching may
    The shining emblem of a life-design decree.

53.
Lyrical Response to a Verse in Sura 17
"The Children of Israel"

55. . . . And We preferred some of the Prophets above others, and unto David We gave the Psalms.

    The Hebrew scriptures have components three:
    The Torah, or Mosaic lore; then next,
    The Prophets; finally, the Writings' text—
    Profusion rich in high variety.

    The Psalm Book? Never called a prophecy,
    Nor David named a sacred Messenger
    As Jeremiah and Isaiah were.
    The godly honor came surprisingly:

    For Íslam, David is a Prophet, plus
    (Advantage ample to appeal to us)
    A hymn-lent herald given added grace:

    A Poet, he attains a favored place.
    We hear his joy and sorrow, cloud and sun,
    As in "'He Frowned,'" or "The Enshrouded One."

54.
Lyrical Response to Verses in Sura 17 "The Children of Israel"

89. And verily We have displayed for mankind in this Qur'ân all kinds of similitudes, but most of mankind refuse aught save disbelief.
90. And they say: We will not put faith in thee till thou cause a spring to gush forth from the earth for us;
91. Or thou have a garden of date-palms and grapes, and cause rivers to gush forth therein abundantly;
92. Or thou cause the heaven to fall upon us piecemeal, as thou hast pretended, or bring Allah and the angels as a warrant;
93. Or thou have a house of gold; or thou ascend up into heaven, and even then we will put no faith in thine ascension till thou bring down for us a book that we can read. Say (O Muhammad): My Lord be glorified! Am I aught save a mortal messenger?

The Master of Similitude
Can see the humor in the feud:
What doubters want He glad outpours,
Yet meanings will the man elude.

The heart it is that spring adores;
The soul resplendent heav'nward soars;
By more than dates and grapes are fed
Blest minds alive to metaphors.

The heav'n comes down, the angels led
To house of gold engarlanded,
The home of him or her that learns
What quick similitudes have said.

The life-despiser, riled, who spurns
The vital fire and sighing turns
Away his rudeness will have rued:
He sullen and unnourished yearns.

55.
Lyrical Response to Verses in Sura 17 "The Children of Israel"

89. And verily We have displayed for mankind in this Qur'ân all kinds of similitudes, but most of mankind refuse aught save disbelief.
90. And they say: We will not put faith in thee till thou cause a spring to gush forth from the earth for us;
91. Or thou have a garden of date-palms and grapes, and cause rivers to gush forth therein abundantly;
92. Or thou cause the heaven to fall upon us piecemeal, as thou hast pretended, or bring Allah and the angels as a warrant;
93. Or thou have a house of gold; or thou ascend up into heaven, and even then we will put no faith in thine ascension till thou bring down for us a book that we can read. Say (O Muhammad): My Lord be glorified! Am I aught save a mortal messenger?

    The God-names, ninety-nine, are mere similitudes:
    He is Compassionate, yet His infinity
    Made that compassion vast in ways that never we
    Will compass, though we can intuit what eludes.

    And of that All-in-One a likeness too am I
    Who in His image am created, one who shapes
    More metaphors by the Divine example. Why
    Await the angels and their palms and dates and grapes?

    One blood-drop is the dawn and sunset and the war
    Of ending and beginning in its metaphor,
    One ganglion the Jacob-ladder in the brain

    When messenger ascending finds unbounded gain
    Of garden where quaternal rivers underground
    Prepare the life stream heard in every fountain-sound.

56.
Lyrical Response to Verses in Suras 17 "The Children of Israel," 30 "The Romans"

17:89. And verily We have displayed for mankind in this Qur'ân all kinds of similitudes. . . .

30:17. . . . His is the Sublime Similitude in the heavens and the earth.

> A sym-bol is together-thrown:
> Two thoughts conjoined, a third is known.
> A meta-phor is borne-beyond:
> We're carried past what all had conned.
>
> A metaphor will farther bear
> The now-unbarred to otherwhere.
> By symbol are together tossed
> Things dísparate, the link not lost.
>
> In symbol one and one combined
> Evolve a third from doubled mind—
> With likeness metaphor will stray,
> Preferring the unlikely way.
>
> The metaphor and symbol are
> A bringer near, a bearer far:
> We bravely travel in the brain
> Expansion, balance, to maintain.
>
> Parabola and parable
> Of that same double-world are full;
> Eccentric and ellipse will curve:
> Before return, we need to swerve.
>
> Messiah, Prophet, Psalmer showed
> The brightness of the likeness-road.
> If God's beyond symbolic reach
> And creatures metaphoric, each,

Of Him, the word must all elude
Of that Sublime Similitude.
He'll teach but as the artist will—
With symbol-image heart to fill.

57.
Lyrical Response to Verses in Sura 19 "Mary"

33. Peace on me the day I was born, and the day I die, and the day I shall be raised alive!
34. Such was Jesus, son of Mary. . . .

76. Allah increaseth in right guidance those who walk aright, and the good deeds which endure are better in thy Lord's sight for reward, and better for resort.

97. And we make (this Scripture) easy in thy tongue, (O Muhammad) only that thou mayst bear good tidings therewith unto those who ward off (evil), and warn therewith the froward folk.

> You'll be more fully guided once you're walking right:
> Good deeds that will endure are best in heaven-sight;
> They form reward whereto for refuge we resort.
>
> God made the Scripture, Prophet, easy on the tongue,
> That you may tidings bear, Remembrancers among,
> The froward warning, swum astray from haven-port.
>
> The day that I was born in peace, the day I die
> In peace, the day I shall be raised into the sky
> In peace affirm: the servant of that Peace am I.
>
> Who hearken to my saying know: a threefold peace
> Can still a rancor-anger in a quick release
> By heart-embracing, that a raging greed may cease.

58.
Lyrical Response to Verses in Sura 19 "Mary"

39. Then she [Mary] pointed to him [Jesus]. They said: How can we talk to one who is in the cradle, a young boy?
30. He spake: Lo! I am the slave of Allah. He hath given me the Scripture and hath appointed me a Prophet,
31. And hath made me blessed wheresoever I may be, and hath enjoined upon me prayer and alms-giving so long as I remain alive,
32. And (hath made me) dutiful toward her who bore me, and hath not made me arrogant, unblest.
33. Peace on me the day I was born, and the day I die, and the day I shall be raised alive!
34. Such was Jesus, son of Mary. . . .

Before he reached the age of sev'n Muhammad's mother died,
The father having left the world before the boy was born.
On many levels of the mind the Prophet may recall
What reawakens now when he of Jesus' life will tell.

For alms and prayer does the latter daily feel ordained:
The Lord has made him dutiful to her that gave him birth.
Should ever he forget this, 'twould be arrogance unblest,
But faithful love will help him gain a never-ending peace.

Remarkably Messiah in the cradle prophesied
What for the early-orphaned son whose mother would be torn
Away would gain the power of a spell: in spite of all
He might endure, a guardian-thought would threat and peril quell.

Muhammad, like his mentor Jesus, healing calm attained
That lent a heaven-blessing to his work upon the earth:
They each 'mid whirling turmoil in serenity would rest,
A never-weakened fervent strength that yearly would increase.

59.
Lyrical Response to Verses in Sura 19 "Mary"

49. . . . We gave him [Abraham] Isaac and Jacob. Each of them We made a Prophet.
50. And We gave them of Our mercy, and assigned to them a high and true renown.
51. And make mention . . . of Moses. Lo! he was chosen. . . .
54. We . . . brought him nigh in communion.
64. We (angels) come not down save by commandment of thy Lord. Unto Him belongeth all that is before us and all that is behind us. . . .
76. Allah increaseth in right guidance those who walk aright, and the good deeds which endure are better in thy Lord's sight for reward, and better for resort.
97. And we make (this Scripture) easy in thy tongue, (O Muhammad) only that thou mayst bear good tidings therewith unto those who ward off (evil), and warn therewith the froward folk.

> To Abraham We Isaac, Jacob gave, and prophet-crown
> Bestowed on each, and mercy, and a high and true renown,
> And Moses have We chosen, for communion coming down.
>
> The angels come not down save by commandment of the Lord:
> To Him belong all things before and those reborn, restored,
> Who lending past to present will expend and never hoard.
>
> The Lord increaseth guidance borne to those who walk aright,
> And deeds of goodness which endure excel in godly sight
> For warm reward, resort in youth and by the latter light.
>
> He made the scripture easy on the tongue, and not a yoke,
> When tidings to the soul you bear, a progress to provoke
> In those who ward off evil, and to warn the froward folk.

60.
Lyrical Response to Verses in Sura 19 "Mary"

61. Gardens of Eden, which the Beneficent hath promised to His slaves in the Unseen. Lo! His promise is ever sure of fulfilment—
62. They hear therein no idle talk, but only Peace; and therein they have food for morn and evening.

Salām, *translated "Peace," has a much wider signification. It includes (1) a sense of security and permanence, which is unknown in this life; (2) soundness, freedom from defects, perfection, as in the word* salīm, *(3) preservation, salvation, deliverance, as in the word* sallama; *(4) Salutation, accord with those around us; (5) resignation, in the sense that we are satisfied and not discontented; besides (6) the ordinary meaning of Peace, i.e., freedom from any jarring element. All these shades of meaning are implied in the word* Islām. *Heaven therefore is the perfection of* Islām. *(A. Yusuf Ali, trans.,* The Holy Qur'ān *780 n2512.)*

> The sixfold gift of peace be with the reader of
> The sura verses that of tranquil Mary tell:
> Each Eden word will from unwearied heart upwell
> To sing of this, the spirit-bliss foretold by love.
>
> Security and flawless, permanent *salīm*;
> *Sallama*, that will rescue and maintain and save;
> *Salām*, our salutation, with a greeting-wave;
> Acceptance and contentment, as may heav'n beseem;
>
> The blending interflow of these will mean release
> From all that might destroy supreme enjoyment: peace.
> We know it here below who've been from rancor freed
>
> And answer, to a deed of ill, a better deed.
> When pardon can a seeming foe to sibling turn
> A garden will we grow and even Eden earn.

61.
Lyrical Response to Verses in Suras 19 "Mary," 20 Tâ Hâ

19:76. Allah increaseth in right guidance those who walk aright, and the good deeds which endure are better in thy Lord's sight for reward, and better for resort.

97. And We make (this Scripture) easy in thy tongue, (O Muhammad) only that thou mayst bear good tidings therewith unto those who ward off (evil), and warn therewith the froward folk.

20:8. Allah! There is no God save Him. His are the most beautiful names.

> The guidance of what's heard inside gave light
> From Origin to those who walk aright:
> Born better for reward and for resort,
> A worthy work finds favor in His sight.
>
> He made the Scripture easy on your tongue
> O Seër, walking wanderers among,
> That you might lead to palm-lined temple-court
> The former froward, by the psalm you've sung.
>
> Right guidance will arrive in speaking plain:
> The ninety-nine, His beauteous names, will gain
> Accumulated strength: defending fort
> Are they in trying time, assuaging pain.
>
> Good tidings bear to those that ward off ill
> And help them live according to His will
> Who over seething sea to haven-port
> Are borne, their heaven-aim adoring still.

62.
Lyrical Response to Verses in Sura 20 "Tâ Hâ"

8. Allah! There is no God save Him. His are the most beautiful names.

9. Hath there come unto thee the story of Moses?

10. When he saw a fire and said unto his folk: Wait! Lo! I see a fire afar off. Peradventure I may bring you a brand therefrom or may find guidance in the fire.

11. And when he reached it, he was called by name: O Moses!

12. Lo! I, even I, am thy Lord. So take off thy shoes, for lo! thou art in the holy valley of Tuwa.

13. And I have chosen thee, so hearken unto that which is inspired.

14. Lo! I, even I, am Allah. There is no God save Me. So serve Me and establish worship for My remembrance.

The meaning of the *mystical* in Greek:
Serenely quiet closing of the eyes
Where million-windowed beauty will arise
For them that rest, who find though never seek.

Of God we saw revealed Mosaic flame,
Harmonious and integral and bright:
The one that favor gained in holy sight
May Consonant, Complete, and Clear proclaim.

Go down the Tuwa valley, where the ground
You touch, and cherish. Let entreating light
That, distant, shivered on the trembling height

Be sign of yet a nigher beauty found
Ungraspable save when the man-eyes turn
Within to see the deep where gleamings burn.

63.
Lyrical Response to Verses in Suras 20 "Tâ Hâ," 75 "The Raising of the Dead"

20:114. . . . And hasten not (O Muhammad) with the Qur'àn ere its revelation hath been perfected unto thee. . . .

75:16. Stir not thy tongue herewith to hasten it.
17. Lo! upon Us (resteth) the putting together thereof and the reading thereof.
18. And when We read it, follow thou the reading. . . .

The light-filled sky, the birded tree,
When left to lie, will perfect be.
The mage when tempted, stirred by haste,
May turn away Eternity.

Indeed, they not in vain have raced
For pardon's sake, with Garden graced,
Who fast to Father-favor sped,
And desert-peril bravely faced—

But they who by the flame are fed
Their zeal mislay and are misled
When spurning time required to wait
Till fire-word fill the heart and head.

The ardor that will mind elate
Combine with drive to meditate:
'Twill be perfected unto thee—
And freedom reconciled with fate.

64.
Lyrical Response to Verses in Sura 21 "The Prophets"

89. And Zachariah, when he cried unto his Lord: My Lord! Leave me not childless, though Thou art the best of inheritors.
90. Then We heard his prayer, and bestowed upon him John, and adjusted his wife (to bear a child) for him. Lo! they used to vie one with the other in good deeds. . . .
91. And she who was chaste, therefor We breathed into her (something) of Our spirit and made her and her son into a token for (all) peoples.
92. Lo! this, your religion, is one religion. . . .
93. And they have broken their religion (into fragments) among them, (yet) all are returning unto Us.
94. Then whoso doeth good works and is a believer, there will be no rejection of his effort. . . .

> The pious Zachariah and his wife upon
> Intense entreaty had been granted baby John
> Who would the Baptist be that helped to lead the way
> To Jesus, heaven-herald, gleaming star at dawn.
>
> The spirit sent to Virgin Mary aided her
> And Jesus, whom, together, heaven would prefer,
> To be for every people emblem, token. They
> Would each of Eden woken be the messenger.
>
> There's one religion, Love—a sun of amity
> One light unbroken shining over ample sea:
> Who such a faith maintain will favor know on high;
> Nor ever may their work and word rejected be.
>
> Receivers of the Baptist proved that they and we
> Could true religion serve with grace-filled rivalry
> In doing worthy deeds. In this then let us vie
> With one another, learning, spurred eternally.

65.
Lyrical Response to Verses in Sura 21 "The Prophets"

106. Lo! there is a plain statement for folk who are devout.
107. We sent thee not save as a mercy for the peoples.

    More plain the statement cannot be for the devout
    That only for a mercy God the Prophet sent.
    Much as for Abraham the flame ascending meant
    A heaven-coolness when the Lord the threat shut out,

    As Lot and Noah rescued were from blaze and rain,
    And Solomon and David had the help of hills
    And birds to hymn, a spell that spirit overspills,
    And judgment-word and jinn-brought pearl and aid would gain,

    As Job received a glory that his woe removed
    And Jonah was rewarded when he could repent,
    And Zachariah, when he prayed that fate relent,
    Was granted John, the son that love for Jesus proved,

    Who then for all the folk was golden token made
    Of mercy that forever in the Lord had lain—
    To all the peoples would the Prophet make it plain:
    Love must from God avail, that grace may never fade.

66.
Lyrical Response to a Verse in Sura 22 "The Pilgrimage"

27. And proclaim unto mankind the Pilgrimage. They will come unto thee on foot and on every lean camel; they will come from every deep ravine. . . .

A pillar of the Muslim faith it is to make
A Meccan pilgrimage and Allah there adore—
Yet those at home can travel, too, that simply take
The perfect journey as a working metaphor.

Respond to the Qur'an, each day one lesson more.
I love to open it at random: day will break
In unawaited ways and light of soul restore,
That I, to be in mind a pilgrim, might awake.

The truths are one, and Love will many rays outpour:
A poor-due, aid to others, for the Heaven's sake,
That vast imagining can lend so I may soar.

The pure and chosen lines illumine the opaque
Within my heart. So turned *kaleidoscope* the ore
New-forged is metamorphic, jewel-forming lore.

The globe not circling, yet I turn a world-of-hues,
A constellation-patterned universe of mind
Creating every moment. I am unconfined
And so, rejuvenescent, no attunement lose.

Yet when the colors of that cosmic thought unbind
A feeling-sequence viewer never can refuse,
In gray and pink of brain the heated golds-and-blues
Unfolding as the heaven-images unwind,

I'm dizzied and I whirl. So Rumi had designed
An art for Sufis: we the *gyroscope* might use
To illustrate the speedy turning, yet entwined

In tranquil balance that the rapid movement views
With calm stability in paradox aligned
To stir a swirling world emerging, heart-enshrined.

67.
Lyrical Response to Verses in Sura 23 "The Believers"

79. And He it is Who hath sown you broadcast in the earth, and unto Him ye will be gathered.

96. Repel evil with that which is better. . . .

>Repel the bad with what is better. We have sown
>You broadcast in the earth, a seed from heaven thrown
>Upon a barren place, fit challenge to create:
>Replace with Eden grace what long ago had flown.
>
>Supplied with light divined above, a hero-fate
>You may be granted, Abram-angels at the gate
>Appear—to aid you, that you needn't go alone:
>The gleaming flame from clay encasing liberate.
>
>From ages gone a saying hard to me is known
>Of water, sudden, coming up from stubborn stone.
>Who Laila's name will write in sand felicitate:
>Mad lover made immortal bard in passion-moan.
>
>They serve not word and world who only stand and wait
>For scroll or tablet graven, golden angel-plate.
>The writ recite within: the scripture make your own
>Implanted in your soul by Him of high estate.

68.
Lyrical Response to Verses in Suras 23 "The Believers," 25 "The Criterion"

23:96. *Repel evil with that which is better.* . . .

25:70. . . . *[He] who repenteth and believeth and doth righteous work; as for such, Allah will change their evil deeds to good deeds. Allah is ever Forgiving, Merciful.*
71. *And whosoever repenteth and doeth good, he verily repenteth toward Allah with true repentance.* . . .

75. *They will be awarded the high place forasmuch as they were stedfast, and they will meet therein with welcome and the word of peace.* . . .

Who'll be steadfast and a true repenter?
One who's learnt the penace-prayer by heart,
Not in mind alone. To mind the center,
Love, compassion, empathy, the art
Consolation mastered, can impart
Guidance to a heaven. Let us enter.

Works of loving kindness are the way
Penitence authentic may be known:
Wasteful both of time and might are they
Who things past and over wail and moan.
Change the bad for better: this alone
Can be *service*: act as when you pray.

Met with welcome and the word of peace
They will be who wakened spirit show
By a higher world of helping. Cease
Vain re-morse—more-biting, yet with no
Added benefit. With God who go,
Freed yet awed, will feel a mind-release.

Ill repel with something that is better.
Pain do not begrudge if you thereby

Spirit gain that underlies the letter,
Mine the text and raise the latter high.
What had stayed away, in faith bring nigh:
Vast imagining—a heav'n-begetter.

69.
Lyrical Response to Verses in Suras 23 "The Believers," 28 "The Story," 41 "Fuṣilat"

23:96. Repel evil with that which is better. . . .

28:54. These [the righteous] will be given their reward twice over, because they are stedfast and repel evil with good. . . .

41:34. . . . Repel the evil deed with one which is better, then lo! he, between whom and thee there was enmity (will become) as though he were a bosom friend.

Matt. 5:44. . . . Love your enemies, bless them that curse you, do good to them that hate you, and pray for them which despitefully use you, and persecute you. . . .

Luke 6:27. . . . Love your enemies, do good to them which hate you,

28. Bless them that curse you, and pray for them which despitefully use you.

All emotions of hatred are bad. . . . But hatred is increased by being reciprocated, and can be quenched by love . . . , so that hatred may pass into love . . . ; therefore he who lives under the guidance of reason will endeavour to repay hatred with love, that is, with kindness. Q. E. D.

 Note: . . . he, who strives to conquer hatred with love, fights his battle in joy and confidence. . . . Those whom he vanquishes yield joyfully, not through failure, but through increase in their powers. . . . (Spinoza, Ethics, Part IV, Prop. XLVI, Proof)

    This page if we might dare to heed
    And follow love, rejecting fear,
    Jew, Muslim, Christian, drawing near,
    Would be of mental fetters freed.

    A few there are who may resent
    A higher strength by self unbound
    And good repay, in will unsound,
    With hate insane, their element . . .

    Yet look within: if we who lie
    And name our weaponry "defense"
    And sell it for a "profit," sense

Have, blind, betrayed, awake! For why
Bring death to women, children, men?
Make peace, I plead! If not now, when?

70.
Lyrical Response to a Verse in Sura 24 "Light"

35. Allah is the Light of the heavens and the earth. The similitude of His light is as a niche wherein is a lamp. The lamp is in a glass. The glass is as it were a shining star. (This lamp is) kindled from a blessed tree, an olive neither of the East nor of the West, whose oil would almost glow forth (of itself) though no fire touched it. Light upon light. Allah guideth unto His light whom He will. And Allah speaketh to mankind in allegories, for Allah is Knower of all things.

>A many-leveled Light is fourfold allegory.
>By wick and olive oil, earth's gift emollient,
>A fire, a star, is from and to the spirit sent;
>Glass, liquid in suspension, will enfold the story.
>
>The Lord, appearing in the moment of satori,
>Is imaged, here, by light on light, in upper sky
>Beyond the sphere-enclosure, too: He's low and high,
>Our home and our horizon, first and final glory.
>
>Of earth and heaven wedded let it tell you true,
>The object and the concept, mystical and moral,
>The fire and eye, the lamp and glass an anthem choral.
>
>A sym-bol to the Greek had meant together-thrown:
>Things distant coming near, in loving closer grown;
>The oil and fire and glow are He and I and You.

71.
Lyrical Response to Verses in Suras 25 "The Criterion," 84 "The Sundering"

25:7. And they say: What aileth this messenger (of Allah) that he eateth food and walketh in the markets? Why is not an angel sent down unto him, to be a warner with him.
8. Or (why is not) a treasure thrown down unto him, or why hath he not a paradise from whence to eat? And the evildoers say: Ye are but following a man bewitched.
9. See how they coin similitudes for thee, so that they are all astray and cannot find a road!
10. Blessed is He Who, if He will, will assign thee better than (all) that—Gardens underneath which rivers flow. . . .

84:16. Oh, I swear by the afterglow of sunset,
17. And by the night and all that it enshroudeth,
18. And by the moon when she is at the full,
19. That ye shall journey on from plane to plane.

>They say, "What ails the messenger of God? He's eating food
>And walking in the markets. Why has not an angel been
>Sent down to him, to be a warner? Why is not thrown down
>A treasure? Why for him no paradise from which to eat?"
>Mistaken viewers claim: "You're following a man bewitched."
>Hear how they coin similitudes for him, so they'll remain
>Astray and never find a road. Be Blest Who, if He will,
>Can give you better: Gardens—underneath them rivers flow.
>
>The lucky ones who merit nothing but have been endued
>As have the birds with lyric scripture-homilies within
>A cryptic form where heaven-letters each with triple crown
>For emblem-eye are ornamented ask the exegete
>To keep the comment brief, by poverty to be enriched,
>For God has told us we shall travel on from plane to plane:
>We'll be the afterglow of sunset, moon that light shall fill,
>The night and all that it enshrouds, dawn henna-fingers' glow.

72.
Lyrical Response to Verses in Sura 25 "The Criterion"

45. Hast thou not seen how thy Lord hath spread the shade—and if He willed He could have made it still—then We have made the sun its pilot;
45. Then We withdraw it unto Us, a gradual withdrawal?
47. And He it is who maketh night a covering for you, and sleep repose, and maketh day a resurrection.
48. And He it is Who sendeth the winds, glad tidings heralding His mercy, and We send down purifying water from the sky.

      The morning came: the Lord had spread the shade.
It could have lain there longer had that been His will;
        Before the dawn He would have kept it still.
Yet He'd withdraw it slowly, and we saw it fade.

      The sun had been its pilot, silent guide,
But only slowly timed, arising to the height,
        To amplify the heaven-hoard delight
In gradual advance and long withdrawal wide.

      The night He spread, a covering for you;
And sleep repose, and day a resurrection made:
        The sun may see the plan that He has laid:
New-thought-awaking, changeful to alerted view.

      Unfolding long and low with patient plan,
The quiet preparation; quick, the winds that sing—
        Each herald of a Mercy—tidings bring:
The song of water brought to purify the man.

73.
Lyrical Response to Verses in Sura 25 "The Criterion"

47. And He it is who maketh night a covering for you, and sleep repose, and maketh day a resurrection.

63. The (faithful) slaves of the Beneficent are they who walk upon the earth modestly, and when the foolish ones address them answer: Peace....

And He it is who maketh night a covering for you,
    And sleep repose, and day a resurrection.
They serve their purpose faithfully who walk upon the earth
    And fellow breathers greet in word of peace.

A bird unscrolled, foreseeing dawn, the gold upon the blue,
    Unwritten trope acknowledging protection.
For them an awed solemnity is blent with surging mirth
    Who, strength refreshed, know cloudlight-stream release.

A gentle-outlined houri-face (her eyes out-morninged sky)
    Bends over me, long hair than mercy-dew
Bestirring more when lovingly the sweeping-light caress
    May touch, along with sufi-soft on-breathing.

Whatever's granted me to give, to this alone am I
    Foreordinated, as revealed by you
That have unveiled the dayscape which the drumming blood can bless
    And Eden turn to lyrical enwreathing.

There cannot be a way more aptly to invigorate
    The universal purpose of the air
That would enliven thunder-heart to utter lasting praise
    And feel each atom in a star exploding:

A benediction hallows me to read with new amaze
    Qur'anic silence that will aims declare
Within my nature planted and may tell of high estate
    By heaven-finger writ with hidden coding.

The faithful slaves of the Benevolent walk modestly
　　Upon the green, pert sproutings heard a-bursting:
The rushes prostrate bent before the speaking One when He
　　Swept over them are faint with humble thirsting.

74.
Lyrical Response to Verses in Sura 26 "The Poets"

83. My Lord! Vouchsafe me wisdom and unite me to the righteous.
84. And give unto me a good report in later generations.
85. And place me among the inheritors of the Garden of delight,
86. And forgive my father, Lo! he is of those who err.
87. And abase me not on the day when they are raised,
88. The day when wealth and sons avail not (any man)
89. Save him who bringeth unto Allah a whole heart.

>Because a meditation on the ninety names and nine
>Will aid the mind in widening to see the one design
>That, as the rainbow colors white unstained will unify,
>In emulating names I try to make their likeness mine.
>
>So here when I recite the pray'r of Father Abraham
>Who would extol alone among his folk the great I AM,
>'Tis useful in perusing lines to think how they'd apply
>And so remake for merit's sake the ode and dithyramb.
>
>I hope as well for wisdom and to gain a good report
>In later generations. For reward and for resort
>The Garden-virtues may I then pursue and ask that I
>Be not abased when they are raised who merit Heaven's court.
>
>I'd glad forgive my elders for whatever errors they
>Had made in aiding me, who've done no better in my day.
>Since wealth and pride in family avail not, let me vie
>With all who race for pardon and with heart devoted pray.
>
>High dignity and valor are the gifts I mainly prize
>In Abraham, his vision see before my grateful eyes.
>An angel cooled his martyr-fire, that he no more might sigh
>Who'd shattered every statue that was blacking out the sky.

75.
Lyrical Response to Verses in Sura 26 "The Poets"

83. My Lord! Vouchsafe me wisdom and unite me to the righteous.
84. And give unto me a good report in later generations.
85. And place me among the inheritors of the Garden of Delight,
86. And forgive my father. Lo! he is of those who err.
87. And abuse me not on the day when they are raised,
88. The day when wealth and sons avail not (any man)
89. Save him who bringeth unto Allah a whole heart.

> "My Lord! Vouchsafe me wisdom, to the righteous minds unite me,
> And give to me a good report in later generations,
> The heritage to merit of the Garden of Delight.
> My father pardon. Lo! he is, alas!, of those who err.
> Abuse me not upon the fateful day when they are raised,
> The day when wealth and sons and pow'r avail not any man
> Save him who bringeth unto God an undivided heart."

So prayed our father Abraham. To grateful thought invite me
The outstretched arms of pardon that he spread before the nations,
That veils let fall away before the newly wakened sight;
Let flourish every seedling that the reaper will prefer,
That ears of wheat on field be found, the gleaner-eyes amazed
To see that more will yet remain, who've gathered all they can;
For every day is harvest meant, the ending or the start.

To vie with others in the race fine work to do incite me
The prayers made by Abraham, to give the loved oblations
With gratitude for stir of day and quietness of night,
For sunwarmth in expanded wave and for the winds awhirr,
For psalming in the summer and the blizzard-winter praised,
For dew and rain, a mercy, for the body-mind to span
The matter-spirit living in the servant-hymn of art.

76.
Lyrical Response to a Verse in Sura 27 "The Ant"

40. ... Whosoever giveth thanks he only giveth thanks for (the good of) his own soul; and whosoever is ungrateful (is ungrateful only to his own soul's hurt). For lo! my Lord is Absolute in independence, Bountiful.

Why can we say that gratitude is only for
The good of those who thank? Your heart in love outpour
With bounty unconditional, and not because
You think it due to this one less, to that one more.

The parent, grateful to a child, upon no laws
Need calculate a basis. Every action awes
The father (well I know), his daughter's heart and mind
Eliciting within the spirit high applause.

A Sufi claimed we should be thankful when we find
We're thanking. Fountain-overflows unloose, unbind
The ground that self-absorbed, contracted, parched, and dried,
Must be renewed in blooming, kindred life and kind.

In drive to utter thanks our empathy's applied—
Concentric virtues, they. Deep feeling, magnified,
Like deepened breathing, in and out, will life restore
In psalm and song and prayer, setting care aside.

77.
Lyrical Response to a Verse of Sura 27 "The Ant"

44. It was said unto [the Queen of Sheba]: Enter the hall. And when she saw it she deemed it a pool and bared her legs. (Solomon) said: Lo! it is a hall, made smooth, of glass. She said: My Lord! Lo! I have wronged myself, and I surrender with Solomon unto Allah, the Lord of the Worlds.

She was so deceived by the reflection of the glass floor in his palace (thinking that she was walking through water) that she tied up her skirts, thus baring her legs. . . . It became immediately evident to Solomon that she, the daughter of a jinn (a supernatural spirit) and a mortal woman, had the body of a normal human being. (Annemarie Schimmel, My Soul Is a Woman: The Feminine in Islam, *58)*

Rabia has also been credited with countless miracles: her fingertips glowed like lamps at night, and the Kaaba came toward her when she made her pilgrimage. . . . She . . . hovered in the air on her prayer rug. (Schimmel 35)

> Rabi'a, fingers tipped with flame,
> Who saw the Kaaba sent to her,
> Our airborne heaven-messenger—
> What grandeur in that saintly name!
>
> In Sheba's momentary shame
> Could smitten Solomon aver
> She holy was—a heart astir
> Where sky and earth twin soul might claim—
>
> In part a jinn. Magician, he
> Conversed with insect, beast, and bird.
> Sweet union, frankincensed and myrrhed,
>
> Would these two lovers' wedding be:
> Rabi'a-like, in light and word
> They talked. The hoopoe saw and heard.

78.
Lyrical Response to Verses in Sura 28 "The Story"

44. And thou (Muhammad) wast not on the western side (of the Mount) when We expounded unto Moses the commandment, and thou wast not among those present;

45. But We brought forth generations, and their lives dragged on for them. And thou wast not a dweller in Midian, reciting unto them Our revelations, but We kept sending (messengers to men).

46. And thou wast not beside the Mount when We did call; but (the knowledge of it is) a mercy from thy Lord that thou mayest warn a folk unto whom no warner came before thee, that haply they may give heed.

>Upon the western mountainside
>Where God to Moses would confide
>The high commandment, you were not.
>More generations would abide
>
>Whose lives dragged on for them: they wrought,
>Though troubled, yet with aid. The thought
>Of God's commandment wasn't gone,
>But, heard again, new strength begot.
>
>And so refreshed they wandered on,
>And messengers before the dawn
>That some would know on Sinai rose,
>Betokening the noumenon.
>
>Excluded though you were from those
>Whom God to hear His doctrine chose;
>Yet latter mercy held in store
>Your task: to others to unclose
>
>The learning you had earned—the more
>A sudden hymn unheard before
>By those untaught and open to
>The light a spirit may restore.

The past had well instructed you
In journeying: the realm wherethrough
You traveled secrets wouldn't hide
That now you let the people view.

79.
Lyrical Response to Verses in Suras 28 "The Story," 66 "Banning"

28:9. And the wife of Pharaoh said: (He will be) a consolation for me and for thee. Kill him [Moses] not. Peradventure he may be of use to us, or we may choose him for a son. . . .

66:11. And Allah citeth an example for those who believe: the wife of Pharaoh when she said: My Lord! Build for me a home with thee in the Garden, and deliver me from Pharaoh and his work, and deliver me from evildoing folk. . . .

> The Prophet, so a memoir narrative relates,
> Told one who wished to fight in battle: Best remain
> To aid your mother; serving her's the greater gain.
> The paradisal garden's at her feet. He states
>
> That Pharaoh's wife had mercy on the Hebrew boy
> And cared for him when hidden, also bringing near
> Young Moses' mother for a nurse. Defying fear,
> The queen converted, and adored the Lord in joy.
>
> I love to picture Moses watched by mothers twain:
> Asíya, kindly-minded; wise Yokhéved, nurse;
> At one in heart and in conviction. Patience waits:
>
> Let heaven-grace the stranger ways of fate explain.
> The orphaned Prophet would his thought in God immerse:
> Mosaic faith will burst Egyptian prison gates.

80.
Lyrical Response to Verses in Sura 30 "The Romans"

22. And of His signs is this: He created for you helpmeets from yourselves that ye might find rest in them, and He ordained between you love and mercy. . . .
23. And of His signs is your slumber by night and by day, and your seeking of His bounty. . . .
24. And of His signs is this: He showeth you the lightning for a fear and for a hope. . . .
25. And of His signs is this: the heavens and the earth stand fast by His command. . . .
27. . . . His is the Sublime Similitude in the heavens and in the earth.

46. And of His signs is this: He sendeth herald winds to make you taste His mercy, and that the ships may sail at His command, and that ye may seek His favour, and that haply ye may be thankful.

58. Verily We have coined for mankind in this Qur'ân all kinds of similitudes.

>The daily goal that will the poet-mind revive
>Is here portrayed—then let me, emulating, strive
>To summarize the guide whereby, Similitude
>Sublime approaching, soul by sense may come alive.
>
>Our love and mercy, fear and hope, awakened mood
>Alert to likeness make; emotions blend or feud
>By night or day; of contrast and of standing fast
>The altered thoughts arise, with life-surprise endued.
>
>Horizon-change and centeredness let be the clue
>To fullness and diversity, extended view.
>To ships the herald winds commended, that will bring
>
>The motive strength to journey—let their heralding
>Be sign of widened range, on vigor-wing desire
>To bear through ocean air: to the Sublime aspire.

81.
Lyrical Response to a Verse in Sura 30 "The Romans"

27. . . . His is the Sublime Similitude in the heavens and in the earth.

Prophetic speech is heaven-height;
In poet-soul will be construed
By metaphors of colored light
The one Sublime Similitude.

From spectrum we expect the white:
The iridescent bow bedewed
Brings riant hope of holy might,
The one Sublime Similitude.

It is a gift, not ours by right,
This plural world, diversely hued:
Find bodily and spirit-sight
The one Sublime Similitude.

Combining modes of dark and bright
Above, below what's human-viewed,
Move nigher to the benedight,
The one Sublime Similitude.

By apathy made tired and trite
Expression may the self elude
That, languid, scarcely dare invite
The one Sublime Similitude.

I beg that morning, noon, and night
Lend ever new-aborning mood:
Transcends apparent blithe-and-blight
The one Sublime Similitude.

The singer will decline to fight
And turn aside from certain feud:
By likenesses can love requite
The one Sublime Similitude.

Imaginers withstand affright
When death approaches, who have rued
No moment, hoping to recite
The one Sublime Similitude.

82.
Lyrical Response to Verses in Sura 31 "Luqmân"

18. Turn not thy cheek in scorn toward folk, nor walk with pertness in the land. Lo! Allah loveth not each braggart boaster.
19. Be modest in thy bearing and subdue thy voice. Lo! the harshest of all voices is the voice of the ass.

22. Whosoever surrendereth his purpose to Allah while doing good, he verily hath grasped the firm hand-hold. Unto Allah belongeth the sequel of all things.

34. Lo! Allah! With Him is knowledge of the Hour. He sendeth down the rain, and knoweth that which is in the wombs. No soul knoweth what it will earn to-morrow, and no soul knoweth in what land it will die. . . .

>Who walk with pertness in the land
>Or turn a cheek to folk in scorn
>With harsh commanding braggart-laugh
>Know not the whence of pelting rain
>Or what is growing in the womb:
>What will your soul tomorrow earn?
>And in what country will it die?
>
>Who persevere with even hand,
>With modest bearing go each morn
>To spend their time on love's behalf
>And put aside the thought of gain
>Nor pow'r to judge a friend assume,
>The better part of life will learn
>And look beyond the single I.
>
>The stork, who'll wingbreadth wide expand,
>A holy minaret at morn
>Can recognize for banner-staff
>And grateful nesting place attain:
>The allegory may illume
>The way we strayers home return,
>Our path well guided in the sky.

83.
Lyrical Response to a Verse in Sura 31 "Luqmân"

27. And if all the trees in the earth were pens, and the sea, with seven more seas to help it, (were ink), the words of Allah could not be exhausted. . . .

They one and all are pens, the trees,
And ink has filled the seven seas,
The liquid kindred to the bough
We hear in wind-breath symphonies

That branches write on troubled sky.
Drop maritime we magnify
Which tiny creatures will allow
The wonder-stunned and ravished eye

As fine-drawn miracle to view;
Translucent ink of myriad hue
In ocean wave each moment now
Made brilliant by the gold-and-blue—

The trees are pens, the seas are ink:
The racing brain won't cease to think
Of Him that wrote, we can't know how,
Nine heavens in the gray-and-pink.

84.
Lyrical Response to Verses in Sura 32 "The Prostration"

15. Only those believe in Our revelations who, when they are reminded of them, fall down prostrate and hymn the praise of their Lord, and they are not scornful,
16. Who forsake their beds to cry unto their Lord in fear and hope, and spend of that We have bestowed on them.
17. No soul knoweth what is kept hid for them of Joy, as a reward for what they used to do.

>The contrasts brought together set awhirl the mind:
>The fallen-down prostration in humility,
>The hymn of praise, and then the frightened cry that we
>Must feel can threaten hope, a groping power, blind,
>
>Then next, the giving-impulse, open-handed, kind,
>To spend of what the Lord bestowed, and so to free
>The deed, the will to give, from chilling fear and be
>Made faint with bliss yet hidden, prize on high designed.
>
>Forsaken beds betoken worry strange, unknown;
>Awareness of reward bespoken, nearer grown
>To one that woke from sleep to heed a great behest
>
>That would transcend the solace trivial of rest:
>Arousal, reassurance, fitful dreams, and care
>Are hallowed—sanctity pervades the turbid air.

85.
Lyrical Response to Verses in Sura 33 "The Clans"

45. O Prophet! We have sent thee as a witness and a bringer of good tidings and a warner.
46. And as a summoner unto Allah by His permission, and as a lamp that giveth light.

> We have sent thee as a witness and a bringer of good tidings
>   and a warner,
> And a summoner to God by His permission, and a lamp that
>   giveth light.
> Let our human creature learn: for truth enduring be a yearner,
>   not a scorner,
> For the finder of the love that is Our life is ever comely in Our
>   sight.
> May the lonely soul arise from her prostration, never more to
>   be a mourner;
> Let the Lord Who is the Daybreak raise the yearners of the
>   world from ancient night.
>
> When We resurrect the dawn We reawake the flame-begotten
>   red beginning,
> Reascending sun a miracle appearing as upon the day of birth;
> May a heart with light beflooded turn aside the straying spirit-
>   whim from sinning:
> Let the warming glory overwhelm a tale of desolation and of
>   dearth;
> For the race to do good work, to gain forgiveness from the
>   height, is worth the winning:
> Sons of heaven, hear your God-belauding hymn resung by
>   children of the earth!

86.
Lyrical Response to a Verse in Sura 33 "The Clans"

63. Men ask you of the Hour. Say: The knowledge of it is with Allah only. What can convey (the knowledge) unto thee? It may be that the Hour is nigh.

    Men ask you of the Hour.
    If it be true that God alone
    Can say the time the wheat-field sown
    Will witness give that it has grown
    To such a height the load when shown
    May far by myriad sheaves be known
        Let souls await their pow'r.

    This knowledge who'll convey?
    The minute, it may be, is nigh
    When we a sign from out the sky
    With heightened heartbeat will espy
    And hymn the art of One on high
    Who sent the rain and sun, that I
        May praise Awaking Day.

    The Hour indeed is here
    For seërs who at daybreak pray,
    Receiving, feeling every ray
    That bears our heavy care away
    Our labor will itself repay,
    Accepting of the heaven-sway
        That to prophetic ear

    Proclaims the moment Now
    When men and women loudly sing
    To laud the hid Creator King
    And Him their tribute grateful bring
    Of heartfelt holy harvesting
    And overswept by spirit-wing
        Bend down and prostrate bow.

87.
Lyrical Response to Verses in Suras 33 "The Clans," 34 "Saba"

33:72. Lo! We offered the trust unto the heavens and the earth and the hills, but they shrank from bearing it and were afraid of it. And man assumed it. Lo! he hath proved a tyrant and a fool.

34:12. And unto Solomon (We gave) the wind, whereof the morning course was a month's journey and the evening course a month's journey, and We caused the fount of copper to gush forth for him, and (We gave him) certain of the jinn who worked before him by permission of his Lord. . . .
14. And when We decreed death for him, nothing showed his death to them save a creeping creature of the earth which gnawed away his staff. And when he fell the jinn saw clearly how, if they had known the unseen, they would not have continued in despised toil.

> Lo! We had offered trust to heavens, earth, and hills,
> But they had shrunk from bearing it—they were afraid.
> And man, assuming it, proved tyrant and a fool.
> When Solomon We gave the wind in strength arrayed,
>
> The blast that, morn or eve, a month-long journey made,
> Outdistancing the very jinn with speed that thrills,
> Did then the king expose to lasting ridicule
> The might We granted, by their labors heavy-laid?
>
> The creeping creature that had gnawed the royal staff
> Evoked from spirits overtasked a languid laugh:
> They wished that they had known from work that they despised
>
> They'd very soon be freed, but they were quite surprised.
> Until man faithfully a steward-role fulfills
> He cannot thrive or prosper; brief will be his rule.

88.
Lyrical Response to a Verse in Sura 33 "The Clans"

72. Lo! We offered the trust unto the heavens and the earth and the hills, but they shrank from bearing it and were afraid of it. And man assumed it. Lo! he hath proved a tyrant and a fool.

I sat beneath a tree for shelter from the heat
And asked: What lack of trust? What shrinking back in fear?
Sweet Eden-wafting breezes rocked in solace dear,
The earth in wreathing green of soothing cool to greet.

I heard, in myrrhal morning, birds adorning air
With arabesque embellishment, to startled ear
Prophetic of the bridegroom from his bedtime cheer
Awaking to the dew-bloom, heaven-wedded, fair.

I gazed upon a cloud whose dawnlight-streaming locks
Had favored me with angel-tresses on my walks...
What timid, unreplying creature turned away?

The earth and sky are trusting—these will ever stay
Obedient, attentive, wakeful, and alert.
But man—if steward of misrule—the world can hurt.

The panoplies of animal and plant protect
Themselves, their young, their comrades, nor a duty shirk.
But humans, welcomed to create a wisdom-work
And use their gift unique, a choosing intellect,

From light of kindness turn away and live in murk
When, as with Solomon, who overdrove the jinns,
In pride of might our grasping Adam-self begins
To enter Iblis where the bloated egos lurk.

The cloud and bird and tree and plant the Lord allow
To guide them in the quiet. Grasses prostrate bow
Before the holy wind, devout in morning pray'r.

But we, who chose to choose, to be aware, neglect
Our fellows in the elements, from faith deféct:
We heat the sea, lay waste the field, pollute the air.

89.
Lyrical Response to a Verse in Sura 33 "The Clans"

72. Lo! We offered the trust unto the heavens and the earth and the hills, but they shrank from bearing it and were afraid of it. And man assumed it. Lo! He hath proved a tyrant and a fool.

> Is humanity at last the master of
> All creation? Cunning, strength, and strategy
> We have known, but Trust contains a realm above
> What we've done. Misguided rationality
> Reason turned to madness. God commands that we
> Learn our Stewardship at last, and practice Love.
>
> We recall the Prophet's holy color: green.
> Healthy alchemy the leaves of trees outbreathe:
> Nourishing our lives and theirs, the gift serene
> Every nature can with vital grace enwreathe;
> Bombs, in contrast, that with devil-rancor seethe,
> Soil the air with poison, turn it base and mean.
>
> God in Mercy to the world the Prophet lent
> Bearing pardon as the mercy-dew and kind.
> Air-polluters who have serpent-venom sent
> Acid rain and ashes for reward will find.
> We for Stewardship, Compassion are designed:
> This the Tree of Life in Eden-Garden meant.

90.
Lyrical Response to Verses in Sura 34 "Saba"

12. And unto Solomon (We gave) the wind, whereof the morning course was a month's journey and the evening course a month's journey, and We caused the fount of copper to gush forth for him, and (We gave him) certain of the jinn who worked before him by permission of his Lord. And such of them as deviated from Our command, them We caused to taste the punishment of flaming fire.
13. They made for him what he willed: synagogues and statues, basins like wells and boilers built into the ground. Give thanks, O House of David! Few of my bondmen are thankful.
14. And when We decreed death for him, nothing showed his death to them save a creeping creature of the earth which gnawed away his staff. And when he fell the jinn saw clearly how, if they known the unseen, they would not have continued in despised toil.

> To Solomon we gave the wind, whereof the morning course
> And that of evening month-long journeys were. Outpouring force
> Of copper ore gushed forth for him, the man was near-bejinned:
> *A worm that bit a staff undid the master of the wind.*
>
> The spirits of the flame by the permission of his Lord
> Made synagogue and statue, basin, boiler, for they warred
> Against the elements in toil, but had the wizard sinned?
> *A worm that bit a staff undid the master of the wind.*
>
> The jinn had been commanded the design and vast desire
> To serve that led King Solomon yet higher to aspire:
> The wealth of Sheba he'd excel and rival that of Ind;
> *A worm that bit a staff undid the master of the wind.*
>
> But penalties were tasted of the unabating flame:
> There's worry in the mind arising: was the king to blame?
> Did some perceive the wild avenger leering as he grinned?
> *A worm that bit a staff undid the master of the wind.*
>
> Be thankful, House of David: bondmen all must grateful be—
> Who serve the Lord in virtue praise will gain eternally.

Yet was it hell or heaven sounds that from the foundries dinned?
A worm that bit a staff undid the master of the wind.

When God decreed his death, a creeping creature of the earth
That gnawed the rod lent question to the deemed supernal worth
Of him who'd kept the burdened worker worried and chagrin'd:
A worm that bit a staff undid the master of the wind.

They realized—the jinns—if they'd envisioned the unseen,
They wouldn't have continued jobs they wished to contravene:
The symbols of the little thing and wicked king are twinned.
A worm that bit a staff undid the master of the wind.

The haughty walking tall are flawed and awful is their fate;
The quelling of their spell will prove the ruin of the great.
What moral law commands can never royal sword rescind:
A worm that bit a staff undid the master of the wind.

91.
Lyrical Response to Verses in Sura 34 "Saba"

34. And We sent not unto any township a warner, but its pampered ones declared: Lo! we are disbelievers in that which ye bring unto us.
35. And they say: We are more (than you) in wealth and children. We are not the punished.
36. Say (O Muhammad): Lo! my Lord enlargeth the provision for whom He will and narroweth it (for whom He will). But most of mankind know not.
37. And it is not your wealth nor your children that will bring you near unto Us, but he who believeth and doeth good (he draweth near). As for such, theirs will be twofold reward for what they did, and they will dwell secure in lofty halls.
46. Say (unto them, O Muhammad): I exhort you unto one thing only: that ye awake, for Allah's sake, by twos and singly, and then reflect: There is no madness in your comrade. . . .
47. Say: Whatever reward I might have asked of you is yours. My reward is the affair of Allah only. . . .
50. Say: If I err, I err only to my own loss, and if I am rightly guided it is because of that which my Lord had revealed unto me. Lo! He is Hearer, Nigh.

Wherever was a warner sent, the pampered ones declared:
"Lo! we are disbelievers in the teaching you've prepared.
As more than you in wealth and children, why should we have cared?"

Say then, Muhammad, "Lo! my Lord will narrow or increase
Provision as He will. Not wealth or children help release
The spirit from defeat until your heightened pride-might cease."

The ones who will believe and good pursue He draweth near;
A double gift to such as these from heaven will appear:
Secure in lofty hall they dwell, know neither grief nor fear.

Awake by twos and singly. Think: your comrade isn't mad.
Whatever he had asked of you, by you it shall be had;
The Lord's reward alone can make the thoughtful Prophet glad.

Say: if I err, let any loss redound to me alone;
If I am rightly guided, let your gratitude be known
To God, the Near, the Hearer, Who to man had wisdom shown.

92.
Lyrical Response to Verses in Sura 35 "The Angels"

27. Hast thou not seen that Allah causeth water to fall from the sky, and We produce therewith fruit of divers hues; and among the hills are streaks white and red, of divers hues, and (others) raven-black;
28. And of men and beasts and cattle, in like manner, divers hues? The erudite among His bondmen fear Allah alone. Lo! Allah is Mighty, Forgiving.
29. Lo! those who read the Scripture of Allah, and establish worship, and spend of that which We have bestowed on them secretly and openly, they look forward to imperishable gain.

These wonderful colours and shades of colours are to be found not only in vegetation but in rocks and mineral products. There are the white veins of marble and quartz or of chalk, the red laterite, the blue basaltic rocks, the ink-black flints. . . .
The Holy Qur'ān: Text, Translation, Commentary *by A. Yusuf Ali, p. 1161 n3911.*

> The blue basaltic rocks, the ink-black flints,
> White marble-vein, red laterite are hints:
> Look forward to imperishable gain
> When reading Scripture-vision symbol-tints.
>
> The berries' ripened-bright enamel-stain,
> The gourds that painter-palette-skill attain,
> The striped and stippled autumn apple views
> Are crafted by the wedded earth and rain.
>
> For cattle, birds, and men divergent hues
> The beauty of our worldscape will perfuse:
> On furry beast and creature of the sea
> Attractive splendor and protective ruse.
>
> Contrastive pigments, too, of you and me
> Allow a shining-colored eye to see
> What will a richly dowered mind convince
> It is the tingeing of divinity.

93.
Lyrical Response to Verses in Sura 37 "Those Who Set the Ranks"

83. And lo! of this persuasion verily was Abraham
84. When he came unto his Lord with a whole heart;
85. When he said unto his father and his folk: What is it that ye worship?
86. Is it a falsehood—gods beside Allah—that ye desire?
87. What then is your opinion of the Lord of the Worlds?
88. And he glanced a glance at the stars
89. Then said: Lo! I feel sick!
90. And they turned their backs and went away from him.
91. Then turned he to their gods and said: Will ye not eat?
92. What aileth you that ye speak not?
93. Then he attacked them, striking with his right hand.
94. And (his people) came toward him, hastening.
95. He said: Worship ye that which ye yourselves do carve
96. When Allah hath created you and what ye make?
97. They said: Build for him a building and fling him in the red-hot fire.

First Abraham unto his Lord
Had come: his love might none divide;
Then, to his father and his folk:
"What do you worship?" he inquired.

"Is it a falsehood—gods beside
The One, Alláh—you have desired?
Behold how sky and earth accord:
Won't this the Lord of Worlds evoke?"

A glance he darted toward the stars,
Then said: "I'm feeling sick!" They turned
And quickly went away from him.
Reply from "gods" he'd next demand:

"Will you not eat? What illness mars
Your will to speak?" And with his hand

He smote them. Foes, their vision dim,
Approached him, and their fury burned.

"You worship what yourselves may carve
When God has made both it and you?"
They said: "A building build, and fling
The rebel in the red-hot fire."

The heart in pride itself will starve
That turned from higher strength its view:
Not self-begot will prophet sing
But voiced by One Who'll joy inspire.

94.
Lyrical Response to Verses in Sura 37
"Those Who Set the Ranks"

139. And lo! Jonah verily was of those sent (to warn)
140. And he fled unto the laden ship,
141. And then drew lots and was of those rejected;
142. And the fish swallowed him while he was blameworthy;
143. And had he not been one of those who glorify (Allah)
144. He would have tarried in its belly till the day when they are raised;
145. Then We cast him on a desert shore while he was sick;
146. And We caused a tree of gourd to grow above him;
147. And We sent him to a hundred thousand (folk) or more
148. And they believed, therefor We gave them comfort for a while.

> Lo! Jonah was among the ones We sent to warn,
> And when he fled, ashamed, to ready-laden ship
> And was of those rejected when the lots were drawn,
> And when he, blamable, was swallowed by the fish,
> Had he not been of those who glorify the Lord,
> He'd there have tarried till the day when they are raised.
> We cast him on a desert shore while he was sick,
> And over him a tree of gourd We caused to grow;
> We sent him to a hundred thousand folk or more,
> And they believed: We gave them comfort for awhile.
>
> At daybreak rise to meet the challenge of the morn:
> Your will make firm, lest waning verve away might slip;
> Enheartened stay by ardent carmine of the dawn,
> And turn to energy the stirring dream and wish:
> A helpful action is inherently reward,
> Completeness felt within outweighing merit praised;
> Let rest converted be to resurrection, quick,
> That by your work the people round you worth may know,
> For wakeful body can the mind to health restore
> When tearful sowers bounty reap with ready smile.

95.
Lyrical Response to Verses in Sura 37
"Those Who Set the Ranks"

139. And lo! Jonah verily was of those sent (to warn)
140. When he fled unto the laden ship,
141. And then drew lots and was of those rejected;
142. And the fish swallowed him while he was blameworthy;
143. And had he not been one of those who glorify (Allah)
144. He would have tarried in its belly till the day when they are raised;
145. Then We cast him on a desert shore while he was sick;
146. And We caused a tree of gourd to grow above him;
147. And We sent him to a hundred thousand (folk) or more
148. And they believed, therefor We gave them comfort for a while.

Called "Dove," the favored "Jonah" hadn't warned—nor flown
Save in the sense of "fled," but overboard was thrown
From off the laden ship where luckless lot he'd drawn,
A bringer of misfortune thought, forlorn, alone.

He, culpable, was swallowed, wonderwork-amazed,
And had he not been one of those who gladly praised
The Lord all breath extols, he would have lingered on
Within that belly till the day when souls are raised.

While he was sick We cast him on a desert shore
And caused a plant of gourd to grow above him tall
And sent him to a hundred thousand folk or more,

And these believed; We gave them comfort after all.
How helpless had he felt below the ocean wave!
Yet down is up when Our beloved son We save.

96.
Lyrical Response to Verses in Sura 38 "Ṣad"

22. And hath the story of the litigants come unto thee? How they climbed the wall into the royal chamber;

23. How they burst in upon David, and he was afraid of them. They said: Be not afraid! (We are) two litigants, one of whom hath wronged the other, therefor judge aright between us; be not unjust; and show us the fair way.

24. Lo! this my brother hath ninety and nine ewes while I had one ewe; and he said: Entrust it to me, and he conquered me in speech.

25. (David) said: He hath wronged thee in demanding thine ewe in addition to his ewes. . . .

Within this valuable parable the seed
You find of gloomy tales of all-consuming greed:
Thus Ahab, though a king, could never be content,
Assailed by gnawing, longing, wanting, craving need.

A vineyard caught his eye, dire envy's maw to feed:
The owner, Naboth, was commanded: Grant it! He'd
Declined. And so the soul was from the body rent:
In stoning-stealing we behold the Thieving Creed.

In Faust, the tyrant-lord of shoreline real estate,
A similar desire climbed high, would not abate:
When Baucis and Philémon had refused to yield
Their home and land and chapel, torment, growing great,

Bombarded Faust. That willful avarice to sate
Mephisto, aiding, came: the couple's tragic fate
Was guaranteed. He killed them. Flaming evil steeled
The coldened heart of those who stole, and ashes ate.

97.
Lyrical Response to Verses in Sura 38 "Ṣad"

22. And hath the story of the litigants come unto thee? How they climbed the wall into the royal chamber;

23. How they burst in upon David, and he was afraid of them. They said: Be not afraid! (We are) two litigants, one of whom hath wronged the other, therefor judge aright between us; be not unjust; and show us the fair way.

24. Lo! this my brother hath ninety and nine ewes while I had one ewe; and he said: Entrust it to me, and he conquered me in speech.

25. (David) said: He hath wronged thee in demanding thine ewe in addtion to his ewes, and lo! many partners oppress one another, save such as believe and do good works, and they are few. And David guessed that We had tried him, and he sought forgiveness of his Lord, and he bowed himself and fell down prostrate and repented.

26. So We forgave him that; and lo! he had access to Our presence and a happy journey's end.

> The man who had the ninety-nine could have no peace
> Until the hundredth of the ewes he had acquired;
> Dire demon greed will grant the seeker no release:
> Who feels that fever is in Iblis' will immired.
>
> But wisdom came to aid the victim who desired
> A respite from the ravage that might never cease,
> The Abel in the tale, whose rabid Cain aspired
> To endless gain and so the guileless liked to fleece.
>
> A message, more than rubies worth, is hidden in
> The deed of David, who had called a halt to sin.
> By judging rightly, for himself as well he taught
>
> How goodness feels—by doing good! And there is nought
> Can let the spirit learn so well to live aright:
> One virtue earns another; habit has that might.

98.
Lyrical Response to Verses in Sura 39 "The Troops"

22. Is he whose bosom Allah hath expanded for the Surrender (unto Him), so that he followeth a light from his Lord (as he who disbelieveth)?

27. And verily We have coined for mankind in this Qur'ân all kinds of similitudes, that haply they may reflect;
28. A Lecture [Qur'ân] in Arabic, containing no crookedness, that haply they may ward off (evil).

>No crookedness, but all made straight and clear,
>Well understood by quick similitudes.
>Yet distance in divinity eludes
>A grasp, a grip: then how to bring it near?
>
>A parable: an indirect, oblique
>Parabola-communication lent
>To clothe in perfect earthly element
>Of poetry what spirit-heart will seek
>
>Above, beyond, below, but only find
>Within, when light and tone in waiting mind
>Have broken ice, a warming-way employed;
>
>Curved, straight combined—capacious life-embrace,
>A vital feeling in upheaval, joyed
>With smiling eyes in long-lost loving Face.

99.
Lyrical Response to Verses in Sura 39 "The Troops"

33. And whoso bringeth the truth and believeth therein—Such are the dutiful.
34. They shall have what they will of their Lord's bounty. That is the reward of the good:
35. That Allah will remit from them the worst of what they did, and will pay them for reward the best they used to do.

>"Remit from me the worst, O Lord,
>Of what I did, and in accord
>With what I've done the best, I pray
>That You reward to me might pay."
>
>No sooner, though, did I request
>A prize for what I thought the best
>Than, mind unblinded, where was fear?
>I felt it, fleeing, disappear.
>
>For when I'd done the best I could,
>I knew I truly understood:
>In doing it the deed was paid;
>No recompense had been delayed.
>
>As for the worst, here too I saw
>The working of a perfect law:
>Your best the bad will cancel: why?
>'Twill ugly anger nullify.
>
>The queller of the evil urge
>As newborn lumen will emerge,
>For if a pride in self can die,
>At length we find a higher I.

100.
Lyrical Response to Verses in Sura 39 "The Troops"

34. . . . That is the reward of the good:
35. That Allah will remit from them the worst of what they did, and will pay them for reward the best they used to do.

    I realize, the more the mind is here immersed,
    The best that I have done itself remits the worst.
    The sacred law of God is graven in the soul,
    As *álif* on the heart (so Háfiz wrote). The first

    Emotion that I feel arose from this: the whole
    Of human body-spirit has, for noble goal,
    The ramified unfolding of entelechy
    That governs leaf and twig and ample branch and bole.

    From up above (a Sufi teacher said to me)
    Will grow, by lofty strength impelled, the spreading tree:
    The potter shaped the urn from upward. So the end
    Of human strength is set by what we cannot see.

    The sun of Spirit shines unviewed, our higher Friend,
    And health of body-mind the human lets attend
    To what promotes unfolding of the total pow'r
    And through the unity of being strength will send.

    By moral weakness heart is deadened by the hour,
    But primal rightness will revive it, and we tow'r
    Above our wayward past; no more remain enhearsed
    In what we've cast away, but welcome health in flow'r.

101.
Lyrical Response to Verses in Sura 40 "The Believer"

36. And Pharaoh said: O Haman! Build for me a tower that haply I may reach the roads,

37. The roads of the heavens, and may look upon the God of Moses, though verily I think him a liar. Thus was the evil that he did made fair-seeming unto Pharaoh, and he was debarred from the (right) way. The plot of Pharaoh ended but in ruin.

    Pharaoh said: "O Haman! Build a tower!
    Then—I will ascend and reach the roads
    Through the heavens: I will never cower
    Gazing on the Moses-God that goads
    Hebrew slaves—through me!—and heavy loads
    Lays on them—when *I* do!—every hour.

    "Truly I consider him a liar,
    Moses, Hebrew leader, and his Lord
    Spoken of as clothed in cloud and fire—
    Sky commander. No! a grander sword
    And an ampler anger wide outpoured
    Serve the King Egyptian, set him higher!"

    So the Pharaoh, sadly led astray,
    Hatched a plot that ended but in ruin:
    God, who'd countermand what he would say,
    Soon indeed would prove the king's undoing,
    Liberated slaves in vain pursuing:
    Foolish man, to choose the tyrant-way!

102.
Lyrical Response to Verses in Sura 41 "Fuṣilat"

34. . . . Repel the evil deed with one which is better, then lo! he, between whom and thee there was enmity (will become) as though he were a bosom friend.

35. But none is granted it save those who are stedfast, and none is granted it save the owner of great happiness.

39. And of his portents (is this): that thou seest the earth lowly, but when We send down water thereon it thrilleth and groweth. Lo! He who quickeneth it is verily the Quickener of the dead. Lo! He is Able to do all things.

Repel the evil deed with one
That's better. See the foe become
As if a bosom friend to you.
Yet none are granted this to do

But steady hearts that fate will bless,
The owners of a happiness,
The portent of their Lord who see:
Earth lowly, growing rapidly

With streams afresh of water sent
To thrill the quickened element
Enlivened by the King of Kings,
Who spurred the yearned-for burgeonings.

The world's a giant hieroglyph
In holy scripture speech, and if
Enlightened by similitude,
No secret key will you elude.

The symbol rooted in your heart
Interpret through bestirring art
And him of self-destructive will
With born-of-bliss forgiveness fill.

Sing *Oro, orior*: so may
Your saying be *I wake, I pray.*
If you are given joy, no less
On "foe" bestow it: friend you bless.

103.
Lyrical Response to Verses in Sura 42 "Counsel"

5. Almost might the heavens above be rent asunder while the angels hymn the praise of their Lord and ask forgiveness for those on the earth. Lo! Allah is the Forgiver, the Merciful.

13. He hath ordained for you that religion which He commanded unto Noah, and that which We inspire in thee (Muhammad) and that which We commended unto Abraham and Moses and Jesus, saying: Establish the religion, and be not divided therein. . . .

    If we can picture Living granted us because
    A loving Being wanted us to utter praise,
    That Love how can we utter? It is bathed in rays
    Of mercy and forgiveness, pardon-heart that awes.

    Blest lives unnumbered may be harmonized in laws
    That are the Noah-dove, the moon-white guiding hand
    Of Moses, lily-raiment loved by Jesus, and
    The tent of Abram that the angels downward draws,

    The time the Prophet rode Buraq above the land
    From Mecca to Jerusalem in wild amaze,
    The high Recital Night that, worth uncounted days,
    Abounded in the glory of the Lord's command—

    The heaven might be nearly rent asunder while
    In psalm of autumn, hymn of spring and winter, we
    Could touch and breathe and feel and taste and hear and see
    The Undissevered—celebrated angel-style.

104.
Lyrical Response to a Verse in Sura 42 "Counsel"

23. . . . And whoso scoreth a good deed We add unto its good for him. Lo! Allah is Forgiving, Responsive.

Forgiving and responsive be
In veneration, for as He
Will add to virtue-deeds you do
More good, redounding bounty we

Expend-expand, replying to
The One Whose guidance can renew
The will to give, and so restore
The strength to plan and carry through

A resolution forth to pour
Abundant horn of plenty, more
Of what we have been granted by
Encouragement to up the score.

Responsive and forgiving I
Can be to self as well where lie
The seeds of inner harmony:
Let heart and mind as partners vie.

105.
Lyrical Response to a Verse in Sura 42 "Counsel"

43. And verily whoso is patient and forgiveth—lo! That, verily, is (of) the stedfast heart of things.

> The dawn that, climbing as with wings,
> Awoke to answer the command
> That's given by the God Who sings
> Within my blood, and can expand
> The soul in song, new hope outflings:
> *Whoever's patient to forgive*
> *Is of the steadfast heart of things.*
>
> The rill that ripples, like the springs
> That nourish, flowing, thirsty land,
> Bright memory of Eden brings:
> Our oversoul will understand.
> I would not trade my state with kings:
> *Whoever's patient to forgive*
> *Is of the steadfast heart of things.*
>
> The babe that to its mother clings
> Will treasured be with tender hand.
> Adorant and accordant strings
> Make fiddler friends a happy band.
> Loved honey's worth the little stings:
> *Whoever's patient to forgive*
> *Is of the steadfast heart of things.*
>
> The quiet earth her burgeonings
> Awaited; she the sky had scanned
> For cooling boon. The raindrop-rings
> On lake and puddle glitter and
> From branch the caterpillar swings:
> *Whoever's patient to forgive*
> *Is of the steadfast heart of things.*

106.
Lyrical Response to a Verse in Sura 47 "Muhammad"

32. Lo! those who disbelieve and turn from the way of Allah and oppose the messenger after the guidance hath been manifested unto them, they hurt Allah not a jot. . . .

> *Yet, with gladdened spirit to surrender*
> *To the pure delight of noble action,*
> *Meanwhile warding off, in thought well-pondered,*
> *Things that only lead to endless torment,*
> *Is the way mistakes may be avoided.*
> *This was written by poor Ebusu'ud,*
> *Be his sins by God in mercy pardoned.*

—J. W. von Goethe, "Fatwa," West-East Divan, *Book of Hafiz*, poem 23 ll.7–13

> He's too big-hearted to be hurt
> Whose mind includes a sky, an earth,
> And proves of deeper, wider worth
> Than what a wrathful man may blurt.
>
> They fight unwisely who assert
> That God is injured ev'n a jot
> No matter what is said and thought
> By idle ire in spiteful spurt.
>
> Therefore has Ebusu'ud said:
> Fear not that one may be misled
> By something written to proclaim
>
> What sober truth may later blame,
> But focus on the lines that guide
> The soul to sky, and high abide.

107.
Lyrical Response to a Verse in Sura 24 "Light"

35. Allah is the Light of the heavens and the earth. The similitude of His light is as a niche wherein is a lamp. The lamp is in a glass. The glass is as it were a shining star. (This lamp is) kindled from a blessed tree, an olive neither of the East nor of the West, whose oil would almost glow forth (of itself) though no fire touched it. Light upon light. Allah guideth unto His light whom He will. And Allah speaketh to mankind in allegories, for Allah is Knower of all things.

    A many-leveled Light is fourfold allegory.
    By wick and olive oil, the earthly element,
    A fire, a star, is to and from the spirit sent;
    Glass, liquid in suspension, will enfold the story.

    The Lord, appearing in the moment of satori,
    Is imaged, here, by light on light, in upper sky
    Beyond the sphere-enclosure, too: He's low and high,
    Our home and our horizon, first and final glory.

    Of earth and heaven wedded let it tell you true—
    The object and the concept, mystical and moral,
    The fire and eye, the lamp and glass an anthem choral.

    A sym-bol to the Greek had meant together-thrown:
    Things distant brought more near, in loving closer grown;
    The oil and fire and glow are He and I and You.

108.
Lyrical Response to a Verse in Sura 48 "Victory"

29. Thou (O Muhammad) seest them bowing and falling prostrate (in worship), seeking bounty from Allah and (His) acceptance. The mark of them is on their foreheads from the traces of prostration. Such is their likeness in the Torah and their likeness in the Gospel—like as sown corn that sendeth forth its shoot and strengtheneth it and riseth firm upon its stalk, delighting the sowers. . . .

Drawn in, the early dew, the mercy-morning fragrance,
I waking felt, spread-eagled, starfished on the grass,
In fantasy new-freed a stirred, alerted vagrance;

The rooted, planted feel of things prayed not to pass
Away, the moveless world that circled and that rolled,
Where all that walk on shifting or on frigid mass

Go upright, all directions up, as we are told
The choiring Torah, Gospel, and Qur'an look high
At once in dark and light, past-future, warm and cold,

Where every quester views a variable sky,
Their eye-directions differing; the whirling fire,
The turning earth, two altered centers that defy

Stability and rest: yet mind and blood and eye
Unite with world and sun, and I on lawn that lie
Know molten core and solar motion, life-desire.

109.
Lyrical Response to Verses in Sura 49 "The Private Apartments"

12. O ye who believe! Shun much suspicion; for lo! some suspicion is a crime. And spy not, neither backbite one another. Would one of you love to eat the flesh of his dead brother? Ye abhor that (so abhor the other)! And keep your duty (to Allah). Lo! Allah is Relenting, Merciful.

13. O mankind! Lo! We have created you male and female, and have made you nations and tribes that ye may know one another. Lo! the noblest of you, in the sight of Allah, is the best in conduct. Lo! Allah is Knower, Aware.

> Suspicion best avoid, for this can be a crime.
> And spy not, neither shall you backbite one another.
> Malignant gossip hides the light and finds the grime.
> Would someone eat the flesh of wept, lamented brother?
> The slander-minded slight the heart, the spirit smother.
> Less worthy than the Serpent they who lie in slime.
>
> A trait that you in ignorance might label bad
> May just be unfamiliar and misunderstood;
> For colorful variety made Allah glad:
> Diversity and contrast He considered good.
> In differentiating gender, tribe, He would
> That empathy be learned, and better times be had.
>
> The noblest, He believed, must be in deeds the best.
> To nation-membership He pays but little heed;
> Take pride not in your birth. Of merit holiest
> Will be the ones that widow, orphan gladly feed,
> Who aid the children and the poor to meet their need,
> Work hard in acts of charity, the moral test.
>
> The slanderer and cannibal are viewed as one;
> Devourers of their kind, they cannot be approved.
> The speaker of an evil rumor is fordone,
> Despite what he may think, by sneaking falsehood moved.
> The man will thrive when having acted as behooved:
> Be all made one by love; suspicion rather shun.

110.
Lyrical Response to Verses in Sura 50 "Qâf"

15. Were We then worn out by the first creation? Yet they are in doubt about a new creation.

16. We verily created man and We know what his soul whispereth to him, and We are nearer to him than his jugular vein.

> More near to you is the creative spirit
> Than jugular that from the head to heart
> The blood, to be renewed, will bring. Restart
> Reborn, for why outworn? The word: we hear it
>
> With every inhalation, counterpart
> To concentration of the force of art.
> Fresh energy take in: they never fear it
> Who form it, bravely shape it and endear it.
>
> More near is creativity than breath,
> My soul has known, and so it whispereth.
> My sole creator yet abides within
>
> As tree in stormwind hides a violin.
> Sweet relaxation is the little death
> Preceding, seeding, what the efforts win.
>
> The streaming freedoms of the coursing red
> That by the breath to hands and feet are led
> You feel in fresh impressions, warm and cool,
> In vivid variation swift outspread.
>
> Proportion is the distribution-rule
> Whereby the body-mind will form a school:
> The chanter allocates the energy
> In atom-rhyme and meter-molecule.
>
> A fearsome wonder shaped, our double tree
> Informs a-borning what we'll make and be:
> By nerves and ganglions of branching fire—
> By artery and vein—we hear and see.

The Leonardo man enclosed entire
Within a globe, symmetric, will inspire:
The bounding and unbounded thus are wed
As blood and air, designed for our desire.

111.
Lyrical Response to Verses in Sura 50 "Qâf"

31. And the Garden is brought nigh for those who kept from evil, no longer distant.
32. (And it is said): This is that which you were promised. (It is) for every penitent and heedful one
33. Who feareth the Beneficent in secret and cometh with a contrite heart.
34. Enter it in peace. . . .

    The Garden is a dream brought nigh
    Of those who kept from willful lie:
    No longer distant, now, the peace
    For which afar was heard the sigh.

    Although the hue and cry increase,
    Yet you in truth can find release
    From strife-bestrewn garrulity:
    Feel portal open, sorrow cease.

    That ev'n the burden fear may be
    A blessing-pledge you secretly,
    If coming with a contrite heart,
    Have learned amid a churning sea.

    We'll death defy when moment-start
    By breath in-taken shapen art
    Will make, from lore of Lord on high,
    An omen, sign, and counterpart.

112.
Lyrical Response to a Verse in Sura 53 "The Star"

32. Those who avoid enormities of sin and abominations, save the unwilled [minor] offenses—(for them) lo! thy Lord is of vast mercy. He is best aware of you (from the time) when He created you from the earth, and when ye were hidden in the bellies of your mothers. Therefor ascribe not purity unto yourselves. He is best aware of him who wardeth off (evil).

>Because the Higher Might is best aware
>Of what we are, and what we were, and where
>We issue, thrice-dark womb where we begin,
>Protected by the long maternal care,
>
>Do not exaggerate the stain of sin
>To dim the wonder Mother bore within:
>Of altered earth and fire divine we're each
>Created, and a paradise can win.
>
>By warding off the ill, we'll Eden reach;
>And it were an abuse of human speech
>In brooding gloom to word unworthiness
>When mercy huge will kind forgiveness teach.
>
>Our hearts not pure, yet purities are less
>Than ardent pardon, for a Strength will bless
>The one who may a synthesis prepare
>Of thought and work, no sin, but heart-largesse.

113.
Lyrical Response to Verses in Sura 53 "The Star"

39. . . . man hath only that for which he maketh effort. . . .
43. . . . He it is Who maketh laugh, and maketh weep. . . .

    The bird that wakened me today at half past five
    Had thrown a frenzied effort into jagged statements
    With up, then down, of sudden turn, in liquid speech,
    For he exhorted me, the sleepy one, to listen.

    The daily effort that to make will keep alive
    The singer 'mid the whirl of unforetold abatements
    And chirping-surges came from One Who glad would teach
    In laughing, crying, what might try, inspire, and christen.

    Recall Mosaic water sprouting from the rock
    As if by mercy-dew of bird-call made to glisten.
    Muhammad saw the Daybreak in a flash, a leap—

    Yet in the desert waste no prophet-bird would talk
    Until to fastness-cavern came the dove. You weep,
    Then laugh, blest friend! Your tear the Seër waked from sleep.

114.
Lyrical Response to Verses in Sura 53 "The Star"

43. . . . He it is Who maketh laugh, and maketh weep,
44. . . . He it is Who giveth death and giveth life;
45. . . . He createth the two spouses, the male and the female. . . .

Three roles—negation, cóntrary, and complement—
In all the pairs above can every member play.
Tears, laughter, death and life, and man and woman may
Conflict, contrast, fulfil each other interblent.

For every two there is a third, a worthy sign:
So tears and laughter in my deepest life combine;
So death and life are shared; nor thought nor flesh the same
As in the mind or in the body when I came.

The androgyne-gynander ever is with me
As life-enhancing as a hidden myth can be:
Since poet is begetter and lends welcome—both,
In writing to transcend them I am nothing loth.

That God be principle of utmost plenitude,
Eternity with time-extension is endued.
Tears-laughter, life-death, woman-man metamorphose:
Kaleidoscopic are the time-forms beauty chose.

115.
Lyrical Response to Verses in Sura 55 "The Beneficent"

26. Everyone that is thereon will pass away.
27. There remaineth but the countenance of thy Lord of Might and Glory.

26. All that is on earth
Will perish:
27. But will abide (for ever)
The Face of thy Lord—
Full of Majesty,
Bounty and Honour. (A Yusuf Ali, trans., The Holy Qur'ān*)*

    When erstwhile earth is empty space
    Will endlessly remain a Face:
    Though God be also as a Light,
    The Eyes than flame have brighter grace.

    A Face will more oppose the night
    Than aught that to our human sight
    In any other metaphor
    Can meaning lend to depth and height.

    A Face that can the rays outpour
    Of gentleness, and life restore,
    By strength and freedom blent to be
    A form creator's blest the more

    The heart envisioning will see
    His many-anthemed majesty
    Where love becomes our dwelling place,
    The heaven-kingdom, inwardly.

116.
Lyrical Response to Verses in Suras 55 "The Beneficent," 56 "The Event"

55:33. O company of jinns and men, if ye have power to penetrate (all) regions of the heavens and the earth, then penetrate (them)! Ye will never penetrate them save with (Our) sanction.

56:74. Therefor (O Muhammad), praise the name of thy Lord, the Tremendous.
75. Nay, I swear by the places of the stars—
76. And lo! that verily is a tremendous oath, if ye but knew—
77. That (this) is indeed a noble Qur'ân
78. In a book kept hidden
79. Which none toucheth save the purified,
80. A revelation from the Lord of the Worlds.

    A Sufi sage had noted that we little know
    Of how the text appeared from which the Prophet read:
    Of parchment, mineral, papyrus—nothing said.
    His penetrating thought, it could appear, would go,

    With angel-aid, to deep Creation-Mind where grow
    The meanings of the universe it was that fed
    Each letter, word, and sentence that the Reader led:
    We ken the Lord by His effects, above, below.

    Similitudes of Him that's hiddden thus will show—
    By things that come to be and may as breath have sped
    Away—what jinns and men may guess when tidings flow

    From likenesses, that eyes in lightning-blaze may glow.
    The poet pure will feel the guiding God, Who wed
    The first and later making, enter heart and head.

117.
Lyrical Response to Verses in Suras 56 "The Event," 57 "Iron"

56:10. And the foremost in the race, the foremost in the race:
11. These are they who will be brought nigh
12. In gardens of delight;
13. A multitude of those of old
14. And a few of those of later time,
15. On lined couches,
16. Reclining face to face. . . .

57:21. Race with one another for forgiveness from your Lord and a Garden whereof the breadth is as the breadth of the heavens and the earth. . . .

> The foremost in the race, the foremost in the race
> Will then recline in Eden, friendly, face to face
> On couches lined, and drink from ewer of a spring
> So fresh in purity as all that sainted place.
>
> There'll be no winner and no loser. To compete
> In amicable zeal for pardon these re-greet
> Their fellow runners in the course illumining,
> Which they are brothers who will follow. Love is meet
>
> Within the universal Garden of Abode.
> The Jujube Tree will spread and bear its heavy load
> Of jeweled fruit and, too, the foliage will cool
>
> Disciples of each other in the Sufi school.
> There, each a whirling *zarra*, we encircle Sun
> With light where perfect wave and particle are One.

118.
Lyrical Response to a Verse in Sura 59 "Exile"

24. He is Allah, the Creator, the Shaper out of naught, the Fashioner. . . .

24. He is God, the Creator,
The Evolver,
The Bestower of Forms
(Or colours). (A. Yusuf Ali, trans. The Holy Qur'ān)

Khalaqa *is the general term for creation, and the Author of all Creation is* Khāliq. Baraa *implies a process of evolving from previously created matter or state: the Author of this process is* Bāri-u, *the Evolver.* Sawwara *implies giving definite form or colour, so as to make a thing exactly suited to a given end or object: hence the title* Musawwar, *Bestower of Forms or Colours; for this shows the completion of the visible stage of creation. (Ali, trans., n3406, 1529)*

> As we're the most developed animal yet known,
> In daily thrice-reborn Creation we are shown
> A microcosmal mirror and *miraculum*
> When tide-made current shapes our wavelet-halidom.
>
> Mind raised from nothingness (in tongue of metaphor),
> I wake, a flow'r unclosed to face the heaven-pour
> Of sun and rain that will evolve a pow'r to grow
> And fully fashioned form and contour later show.
>
> Creator, Fashioner, and Form-Bestower He:
> And so it would behoove our moving soul to be
> In every way we're able, in supreme degree
>
> Permitted when within the narrow human breast
> A room is made, a breadth—from heaven holiest
> (More angels, greater place) blent ray of East and West.

119.
Lyrical Response to a Verse in Sura 59 "Exile"

24. He is Allah, the Creator, the Shaper out of naught, the Fashioner. His are the most beautiful names. . . .

The beautiful attracts, and if the name or *-nym*
We may relate to *nomos*, or the strength of law,
A *nomen* lends a rule that, based on what we saw,
We'd like to emulate—the best belong to Him.

But what gave rise to man-made nam-ing? Can a flaw
Have entered here our thinking based upon a whim?
The force primordial that formed from chaos dim
The world confronting Nothing—may this Lord in awe

Not be denominated "What to Names will give
Whatever Being may enable them to live
When framed by mortal shapers of the oral ore

Whose ear will make them aural and auroral, more
Than ninety-nine times ninety-nine, the holy ones
We mirror in our strophe'd writings' lyric suns"?

120.
Lyrical Response to a Verse in Sura 63 "The Hypocrites"

10. And spend of that wherewith We have provided you before death cometh unto one of you and he saith: My Lord! If only thou wouldst reprieve me for a little while, then I would give alms and be among the righteous.

    And spend of what We have provided you
    Before the time when you must die the death,
    And one of you, on its arrival, saith,
    "Reprieve me for a little while, pray do!

    I'll then give alms and be a righteous man,
    And prove a faithful servant and a true,
    A giver known for charity, and who
    Will grant the needy everything he can."

    Reprieve yourself this minute, save your breath;
    Procrastinators' faded shibboleth
    Cannot avail, or change the fated view

    Of what ungentle doom you're heading to:
    To reach a higher plane, you need a plan;
    Act now, and carry out the blest Qur'an.

121.
Lyrical Response to Verses in Sura 64 "Mutual Disillusion"

16. So keep your duty to Allah as best ye can, and listen, and obey, and spend; that is better for your souls. And whoso is saved from his own greed, such are the successful.
17. And if ye lend unto Allah a goodly loan, he will double it for you and will forgive you, for Allah is Responsive, Clement. . . .

Lucky, rescued from their greed,
Some with heaven-gold succeed.
Wealth is but abundant life,
No investor knowing strife.

Loans to God let given be
Not for profit, interest-free:
Struggle only to complete
Virtue's early hero-feat.

Race for favor from your Lord,
Nor as others, huddled, hoard.
May ill-gotten gain be dropped
And the craven craving stopped.

Doubled be the flood of peace
Heart will feel, and seizing cease;
Let no devil's ire foreclose
Mortgage mortal blindness chose.

Allah will forgive your debt
When you orphan, widow let
Share the wealth He gave in grace:
Abram-angel may you face.

122.
Lyrical Response to Verses in Sura 64 "Mutual Disillusion"

16. So keep your duty to Allah as best ye can, and listen, and obey, and spend; that is better for your souls. And whoso is saved from his own greed, such are the successful.

17. If ye lend unto Allah a goodly loan, He will double it for you and will forgive you, for Allah is Responsive, Clement,

18. Knower of the invisible and the visible, the Mighty, the Wise.

> Your duty keep as best you can;
> Contain the *nafs* or lower man;
> Hoard not your wealth; its farther span
>   You will foresee:
> Unbarred, a starry heart-world scan
>   Wherein to be.
>
> Then listen, and obey, and spend:
> The day begin as if the end
> In fellowship would lesson lend—
>   A way to live
> Emerges when a hidden Friend
>   Will urge to give.
>
> The one delivered from his greed
> Is of the kind that will succeed:
> May "I" not blind—by helpful deed
>   A rose reveal:
> Aroma grow of light-filled seed
>   And sky unseal.
>
> Who lend their God a plenteous loan
> Will find it doubled; not our own
> Are we—pearled mercy-dew bestrown
>   And light-beams 'round.
> Ev'n so have I, the sky-child, known
>   Green Eden-ground.

Now open wide your pensive eyes,
For He, Replying, Clement, Wise,
The hidden, clear, alike espies—
   In dark the light,
As mind revived in time descries
   Recital Night.

123.
Lyrical Response to a Verse in Sura 67 "The Sovereignty"

19. Have they not seen the birds above them spreading out their wings and closing them? Naught upholdeth them save the Beneficent. Lo! He is Seer of all things.

... das Zwitschern der Vögel mit ihren Jungen, für die sie rastlos sorgen bis sie flügge sind. [... the twittering of the birds with their young, for whom they untiringly care till they are fledged.]—Letter from Katharina Mommsen

>They glide in sky, evade the wind-roar chilly-edged,
>Who spread their wings and close them, naught upholding these,
>Unquestioning, directed in their way with ease,
>By parents guided, taught, till they were fully fledged.
>
>May I so birded be in wording, blessing-pledged,
>And skim above the swirl, and 'mid the skirling breeze,
>To ponder, as I fly, compliant melodies
>('Mid acrobatic turns) that with the swampland sedged
>
>In windwhirl blent recall the dervish-fluting reed
>Mevlana praised: how far soever she would roam
>He yet could hear a longing for her godly home.
>
>Till such a time as He the wailing tune may heed
>And cloud shall spread beneath her, smooth and soothing, she
>No melody can lend but Eden-elegy.

124.
Lyrical Response to Verses in Sura 70
"The Ascending Stairways"

3. . . . Allah, Lord of the ascending stairways
4. (Whereby) the angels and the Spirit ascend unto Him in a Day whereof the span is fifty thousand years.
5. But be patient (O Muhammad) with a patience fair to see.

19. Lo! man was created anxious,
20. Fretful when evil befalleth him
21. And, when good befalleth him, grudging;
22. Save worshippers
23. Who are constant at their worship
24. And in whose wealth there is a right acknowledged
25. For the beggar and the destitute. . . .

    Lord of the ascending stairways He:
    Angels and the Spirit in a Day
    Climb it in a period that we
    Feel as fifty thousand ages. Pray,
    Prophet, being mindful of the way
    Time will flow, with patience fair to see.

    Man's created anxious, eager judge
    Of what seems an evil and, if good
    Happen, from the sulkiness won't budge,
    Fretful, having poorly understood
    Time can not be hastened. If it could,
    Some would yet retain a sullen grudge.

    People of another kind there are
    Who are steady in a mental pray'r;
    Constant-minded, these no greed will mar:
    They for beggars and the poor will care
    And in need no aid nor effort spare.
    Climb the stairway: Spirit-wealth unbar.

125.
Lyrical Response to Verses in Sura 70 "The Ascending Stairways"

3. . . . Allah, Lord of the Ascending Stairways
4. (Whereby) the angels and the Spirit ascend unto Him in a Day whereof the span is fifty thousand years.
5. But be patient (O Muhammad) with a patience fair to see.

    Candescent and conclamant seraphim
    The Lord of the Ascending Stairways hymn:
    The angels and the Spirit in a day
    Will move, with speed no human hand may limn,

    The four and twenty hours whereof we may
    In fifty thousand years attain. Then stay
    Content in mortal time while steadily
    You aim your gaze toward the higher Way.

    Be patient with a patience fair to see,
    As God the Prophet counseled. Let it be
    With calm of spreading daybreak that we view
    Similitude supreme for such as we.

    Let angel-gold amid the azure-blue
    The cloudy gonfalon with flame bestrew
    Until the twilight shall the sky bedim
    And night in mercy greening field bedew.

126.
Lyrical Response to Verses in Sura 72 "The Jinn"

In the name of Allah, the Beneficent, the Merciful.
1. Say (O Muhammad): It is revealed unto me that a company of the Jinn gave ear, and they said: Lo! it is a marvellous Qur'ân,
2. Which guideth unto righteousness, so we believe in it and we ascribe no partner unto our Lord.

A company of Jinn gave ear:
"It is a marvelous Qur'an,
Which guideth unto righteousness;
We in the same henceforth believe,
Ascribe no partner to our Lord."

A fire upraised need soul not fear:
They speedily astray have gone
That feel in heat no strength to bless;
Who know not gray will surely grieve,
Yet splendor flaming tongues afford.

To pierce the air with burning spear
When streaming hair the face of dawn
Will shake, ablaze, can faith confess—
Whatever would of grace bereave
Defeated by the angel sword.

Entreated we the Lord: "Appear
Before the seething green of lawn
Be shadowed and the something less
Our understanding hapless thieve
And we become a heedless horde."

Renew the universal year
In moment-thunder: Spirit, spawn
Abundance more than jinn may guess,
And thirsting, rough-erupting heave
The lava-burst within you stored.

127.
Lyrical Response to Verses in Sura 73
"The Enshrouded One"

5. For We shall charge thee with a word of weight.
6. Lo! the vigil of the night is (a time) when impression is more keen and speech more certain. . . .

10. And bear with patience what they utter, and part from them with a fair leave-taking.
11. Leave Me to deal with the deniers, lords of ease and comfort (in this life); and do thou respite them awhile.

    For We shall charge you with a word
    Of weight—to be in spirit heard
    By night when silent heights enshroud
    The one averted, heart-bestirred.

    As though surrounded in a cloud
    Before the wind is prostrate bowed
    The waker, waiting. Soul averred
    Most mighty bliss to him allowed.

    The Lord a quiet time preferred:
    When world-disturbance had occurred
    With brash and brazen clangor loud,
    Whereat the tranquil mind demurred,

    To deeper aim was Prophet vowed:
    More keen at night the speech uncowed,
    Relieved of the denier. Spurred
    To learn, he tried to serve, not proud.

128.
Lyrical Response to Verses in Sura 76 "'Time' or 'Man'"

25. Remember the name of thy Lord at morn and evening.
26. And worship Him (a portion) of the night. And glorify Him through the livelong night.

17. There [in Heaven] are they [the righteous] watered with a cup whereof the mixture is of Zanjabîl,
18. The water of a spring therein, named Salsabîl.

> At morn and eve the names of God recall.
> Though they are nine and ninety, yet of all
> The beings of unnumbered kind the names
> Will mind from finite limit disenthrall.
>
> Each allegoric likeness rightly claims
> A plentitude of metaphoric frames
> That, universal wholeness making known,
> Outshine the *zarras* whirling in the flames.
>
> In twilight, dreaming of the hidden Throne
> At dusk and dawn, dark-light together grown,
> We feel a change in sweet transition-state,
> Our altered nature at His altar own.
>
> Awake in dark at times, to watch and wait,
> We hark, and vigil-stillness cultivate,
> The Lord adoring till it be His will
> That we, in lifted lightness, contemplate.
>
> Then holy praise the heaven-heart may fill
> And we from Salsabîl and Zanjabîl
> The waters then might drink, to our content,
> With what our dithyrambic hymns instill.
>
> And, this occurring, from the World-King sent,
> Euterpal, quintessential element
> Transforming us, we feel by hidden might
> The Place of Refuge where the Prophet went.

We glorify, throughout the livelong night,
The Lord, restored the metamorphic sight
Of any yet encumbered—Father-Hall
Aswim in oneness' never-dimming light.

129.
Lyrical Response to Verses in Sura 78 "The Tidings"

31. Lo! for the duteous is achievement—
32. Gardens enclosed and vineyards,
33. And maidens for companions,
34. And a full cup.

        Achievement for the duteous,
        A vineyard and a garden closed,
        A maiden boon companion pure,
        An Eden cup of ruby fire.

        A friend to chant, compare, discuss,
        A cultivation soul-proposed,
        A zephyr pilgrim for allure,
        A hymned requital in a choir.

        An act by thought rewarded thus,
        By lyric filled, metamorphosed,
        A shaping that can life ensure,
        A rhyming of a spring desire.

        The undertaker's overplus,
        A poem by the heartstring glozed,
        A more than mortal portraiture:
        Mirific wisdom we respire.

130.
Lyrical Response to Verses in Sura 80 "'He Frowned'"

1. *He frowned and turned away*
2. *Because the blind man came unto him.*
3. *What could inform thee but that he might grow (in grace)*
4. *Or take heed and so the reminder might avail him?*
5. *As for him who thinketh himself independent,*
6. *Unto him thou payest regard.*

        The blind abruptly will intrude
        When you would rather see the ones
        Who, glitter-eyed as gleaming suns,
        May suit your bland, expanding mood.

        They humbly ask, the summoners,
        That you be willing guide and show
        The baffled impulse where to go.
        Who turns away, acerb, demurs,

        The rough discomfort may elude,
        But faster he from virtue runs.
        Yet in the night the secret stuns:
        'Tis with my deeper mind I feud.

        The sight that favored gaze prefers
        Denied the living will below.
        Availing not that grace might flow,
        He failed to be the dawn that stirs.

131.
Lyrical Response to Verses in Sura 80 "'He Frowned'"

In the name of Allah, the Beneficent, the Merciful.
1. He frowned and turned away
2. Because the blind man came unto him.
3. What could inform thee but that he might grow (in grace)
4. Or take heed and so the reminder might avail him?
5. As for him who thinketh himself independent,
6. Unto him thou payest regard.
7. Yet it is not thy concern if he grow not (in grace).
8. But as for him who cometh unto thee with earnest purpose
9. And hath fear,
10. From him thou art distracted.
11. Nay, but verily it is an Admonishment,
12. So let whosoever will pay heed to it,
14. On honored leaves
15. Exalted, purified,
15. (Set down) by scribes
16. Noble and righteous.

>You frowned and turned away because the blind man came.
>Had you no hint that, staying, he might grow in grace,
>Availing guidance follow, wayward aim erase?
>The proud one only did you heed, so merit blame.
>
>And ought you not consider how the blind might grow?
>He comes with earnest purpose, and with seemly fear:
>Yet were you culpably distracted. We that hear
>And from that lapse take note, will be instructed so.
>
>Exalted, purified, and honored are the leaves
>Whereon admonitory teaching we may read:
>The reader who'd right-minded be is paying heed.
>
>The scribe, in writing down the story of a flaw,
>Portrayed both human nature and the moral law:
>High parable, through narrative be sad, one weaves.

132.
Lyrical Response to Verses in Sura 84 "The Sundering"

16. Oh, I swear by the afterglow of sunset,
17. And by the night and all that it enshroudeth,
18. And by the moon when she is at the full,
19. That ye shall journey on from plane to plane.

> I swear by lambent sunset afterglow
> And by the night, her silent shrouding pow'r,
> And by the moon when she is at the full,
> That you will journey on from plane to plane.
>
> And through what heav'n soever you may go—
> Where aging star may fall, light-scattered flow'r—
> By stress and then release, by press and pull,
> Your breathing deeper strength shall ever gain.
>
> The meaning of each likeness you shall know,
> To view within the tiniest a tow'r,
> To find in lion, eagle, man, and bull
> The fourfold nature of the heart humane.
>
> Where Eden rivers of the soul may flow
> By tulip-ruby, dewy diamond-dow'r,
> Your wine will bring no sleep residual,
> But aid more deft perception to attain.
>
> Upon the prostrate green that lies below
> The sages' walk in meditative hour,
> Whose feet shall tread on lawn more soft than wool,
> The light will shine of suns that never wane.

133.
Lyrical Response to Verses in Sura 85 "The Mansions of the Stars"

19. Nay, but those who disbelieve live in denial
20. And Allah, all unseen, surroundeth them.
21. Nay, but it is a glorious Qur'ân.
22. On a guarded tablet.

How then to feel the plenitude unseen
About us? How to cure a heart-denial?
Sad habit-apathy: our spirit-trial.
    The clever eye and keen,

However, may reject a burden-weight
Of what had dulled the mind, recurrent yoke
Of blinding custom, and refind the stroke
    Of *álif.* Contemplate

The heart-touch that the soul-Creator made
Who wrote the guarded letter of a love
That is within, below, around, above.
    Who may the load unlade

Of last-year skin as yearly can the snake
Will feel a strength return—so, on the day
When waters parted, Spirit *álif*-way
    Would on their surface make.

Retreat, resile, return, and find the All
Without that you within had silent viewed:
A guarded *Yes* no longer can elude
    The urgent heaven-call.

A UNIFYING LIGHT 157

134.
Lyrical Response to Verses in Sura 86 "The Morning Star"

In the name of Allah, the Beneficent, the Merciful.
1. By the heaven and the Morning Star
2. —Ah, what will tell thee what the Morning Star is!
3. —The piercing star!
4. No human soul but hath a guardian over it.
5. So let man consider from what he is created.
6. He is created from a gushing fluid
7. That issued from between the loins and ribs.

[Note by Pickthall to "Morning Star": The Arabic word meant originally "that which comes at night" or "one who knocks at the door."]

>Reveal: what is the Morning Star?
>Within it, thing and spirit are:
>It comes upon you in the night;
>One knocks—the door unlocked, ajar!
>
>To every soul beholding light
>A guardian is lent, by right
>Of Allah's will, His godly grace,
>A guide in darkness, benedight,
>
>That you may see a human face
>In father and in farther place,
>In earthly and in stellar eye,
>In depth of breath, in ray of space.
>
>Between the loins and ribs doth lie
>The source of gushing fluid. Why
>Will human life aspire afar?
>We're pierced of kindly star on high.
>
>What comes at night and knocks upon
>The door, and will invite the dawn,

Of body, soul at once can tell:
It haunts me and will not be gone.

The fluid, as of Moses' well,
A spirit-miracle will spell,
Prelusive, too, of water clear
And fruits that for the Virgin fell.

A piercing as of angel-spear
The mind to sky-heart will endear:
Like father Jacob, ev'n when lamed,
We fiery love in light revere.

Though made of clay, with them we've claimed
A kinship. Form symmetric-framed
Let's hymn upon the barbiton
And heaven-flute of Rumi famed.

The one a-knocking at the door
And coming in the night, before
The Cleaver of the Daybreak rise,
We call the Morning Star. Outpour

Your meaning-wealth: let shine the eyes
When mind delightedly espies
A threefold analogue, our guide!
Within the Arab tongue there lies

A poetry that has defied
My fathoming attempt—too wide
And deep, too manifold and high.
Unbounded ever you abide.

To ask the everlasting Why,
Let heart be open, so that I
May ponder, wise, the metaphor
And to the Lord in glory fly.

135.
Lyrical Response to Verses in Suras 86 "The Morning Star," 96 "The Clot"

86:5. So let man consider from what he is created.
6. He is created from a gushing fluid
7. That issued from between the loins and ribs.

96:1. Read: In the name of thy Lord who createth,
2. Createth man from a clot.
3. Read: And thy Lord is the Most Bounteous,
4. Who teacheth by the pen,
5. Teacheth man that which he knew not.

>The pen, the fluid, and the clot
>Will teach man that which he knew nót.
>Than God is none more bounteous,
>Conceiving world in single thought.
>
>The One, abundant overplus,
>Though puzzled poets long discuss,
>They never comprehend the source
>That led from nothing unto us.
>
>The might that must be more than force
>Will channel chance in varied course
>Till seed-milk of galactic cloud
>The sperm of all the worlds endorse.
>
>Let me, like grass, be prostrate, bowed
>Before the Forms, that Angel-crowd;
>By fluid, clot, and pen be taught
>What hallowed craft the Lord allowed.

136.
Lyrical Response to Verses in Sura 91 "The Sun"

In the name of Allah, the Beneficent, the Merciful.

1. *By the sun and his brightness,*
2. *And the moon when she followeth him,*
3. *And the day when it revealeth him,*
4. *And the night when it enshroudeth him,*
5. *And the heaven and Him who built it,*
6. *And the earth and Him who spread it,*
7. *And a soul and Him who perfected it*
8. *And inspired it (with conscience of) what is wrong for it and (what is) right for it.*
9. *He is indeed successful who causeth it to grow,*
10. *And he is indeed a failure who stunteth it.*

      The sun is bright; he's followed by the moon,
      Revealed by day, enshrouded by the night.
      The parallels with God our mood attune:
      He heaven built, spread earth, and with His might
      Perfected souls and gave them conscience-light.
      He's in our Sun: for humans, godly boon.

      Whoever will allow the soul to grow,
      Which, like the Lord, is warmth of Sun to me
      And joy of height that, wed to soil below,
      Brings life, the *Fiat lux*, the *Light let be*,
      Is turned to origin eternally,
      The glance that worlds refract in colored bow.

      Whoever, though, will stunt the spirit-growth
      Indeed may ever be a failure named.
      Whoso, with blinkered vision, will be loth
      To let the strength unfold must be ashamed:
      To serve the solar gold of soul unblamed
      Let's turn away from lies and blindness both.

137.
Lyrical Response to Sura 93 "The Morning Hours"

5. And verily thy Lord will give unto thee so that thou wilt be content.
6. Did He not find thee an orphan and protect (thee)?
7. Did He not find thee wandering and direct (thee)?
8. Did He not find thee destitute and enrich (thee)?
9. Therefor the orphan oppress not,
10. Therefor the beggar drive not away,
11. Therefor of the bounty of thy Lord be thy discourse.

Tradition also ascribed to him the beautiful saying "Paradise lies beneath the feet of the mothers." (Annemarie Schimmel, And Muhammad Is His Messenger *51)*

>Though early orphaned, by his uncle raised,
>The Prophet (may the Lord of Grace be praised)
>Had learned the love, a morning star within,
>That Gabriel would make him feel, amazed.
>
>When told to read, he feared it was a jinn
>That summoned, thus entrapping him in sin;
>But he whom none had taught to read a line,
>Lent light of mind, would heaven-doctrine win.
>
>His wife convinced him that a ray divine
>Shone forth in Angel Gabriel, a sign
>That God the man had wanted to portray
>A mercy-life more pure than Eden wine.
>
>In later years, our paradise, he'd say,
>Beneath the feet of loving mothers lay.
>The smiling eyes of him, like sunlight, blazed
>When he, for wife so motherly, would pray.

138.
Lyrical Response to Sura 94 "Solace"

In the name of Allah, the Beneficent, the Merciful.
1. Have We not caused thy bosom to dilate,
2. And eased thee of the burden
3. Which weighed down thy back;
4. And exalted thy fame?
5. But lo! with hardship goeth ease,
6. Lo! with hardship goeth ease;
7. So when thou art relieved, still toil
8. And strive to please thy Lord.

        We caused your bosom to dilate
        And eased you of the burden great
        That weighed and weary made. A fate
        Unprecedented would await.

        For lo! with hardship goeth ease,
        And praising Him your heart will please.
        We feel a storm in cedar trees:
        What He pre-formed will spirit seize.

        Remember then—at last relieved,
        Help widow, orphan, those aggrieved:
        If you an ample gift received,
        Give spring to souls that winter thieved.

        Do not forget this moment: be
        Expender, love-extender. He,
        Our Lord, won't hoard but openly
        Outpour, ungreedy, spirit-free.

139.
Lyrical Response to Sura 94 "Solace"

In the name of Allah, the Beneficent, the Merciful.
1. Have We not caused thy bosom to dilate,
2. And eased thee of the burden
3. Which weighed down thy back;
4. And exalted thy fame?
5. But lo! with hardship goeth ease,
6. Lo! with hardship goeth ease;
7. So when thou art relieved, still toil
8. And strive to please thy Lord.

    Has God not made your breast dilate
    And back of weight relieved,
    That by a burden over-great
    You might not be aggrieved,
    But may in fame and fair estate
    Be placed, as He conceived?
    Then strive each day your Lord to please,
    For lo! with hardship goeth ease.

    The Cleaver of the Daybreak, He
    The henna-fingered Dawn
    Has taught to paint the melody
    Of angel-birds whereon
    The feathered wings you favored see
    That flash upon the lawn:
    Then strive each day your Lord to please,
    For lo! with hardship goeth ease.

    The sun that golden hair will shake
    Impatient of the dark
    A sky more smiling so will make
    To hail the rising lark,
    For them whose thirst the Lord would slake
    With grace He first will mark:
    Then strive each day your Lord to please,
    For lo! with hardship goeth ease.

The raven and the peacock may
Together represent
The aged night, the healing ray
Of spreading daylight sent;
A pair of sacred emblems they
To eager teaching lent:
Then strive each day your Lord to please,
For lo! with hardship goeth ease.

The tulip, daffodil, and rose
Will rise to morning prayer;
I raise my hands in praise to those
That bright-aroma'd air
Have heightened as the eyes unclose—
We feast on fragrance fair:
Then strive each day your Lord to please,
For lo! with hardship goeth ease.

The rubious and Eden wine,
The morning star and bright,
The threshold dust, the more divine
Near lover-eyes alight,
Have waked the soul by hoopoe-sign
Of Sheba's welcome sight:
Then strive each day your Lord to please,
For lo! with hardship goeth ease.

Thus Abraham the clumps and clods
Of clay that some revered
Defied, and knowing well the odds
Against him, never feared
The power of his father's gods
And flames, remaining cheered:
Then strive each day your Lord to please,
For lo! with hardship goeth ease.

When Mary in her labor lay
And unremitting pain,
Behold! a gleaming stream would play,
That drink she might attain,

And wondrous palm-tree down would sway,
That she the dates might gain:
Then strive each day your Lord to please,
For lo! with hardship goeth ease.

When Gabriel the Angel made
The wakened Prophet read
The riddle-script before him laid,
He high command would heed
And chanted, awed, with godly aid
To plant the Heaven seed:
Then strive each day your Lord to please,
For lo! with hardship goeth ease.

140.
Lyrical Response to Sura 97 "Power"

In the name of Allah, the Beneficent, the Merciful.
1. Lo! We revealed it on the Night of Power.
2. Ah, what will convey unto thee what the Night of Power is?
3. The Night of Power is better than a thousand months.
4. The angels and the Spirit descend therein, by the permission of their Lord, with all decrees.
5. (That night is) Peace until the rising of the dawn.

> The Night of Pow'r what will convey
> To them who seek the Lord in day
> Alone? For, though He be the Sun
> In brightness and in heaven-sway,
>
> His dark is kindred to the one
> Of wonder when the deed was done
> Wherein by suprasolar light
> The Angel Gabriel had begun
>
> To let appear the More-Than-Bright
> To Prophet on Recital Night.
> The Lord in metaphor alone
> Can spoken be with poet-might:
>
> By language that we mortals own
> God's nature won't be wholly known.
> Similitude must point the way,
> Analogy to soul be shown.
>
> Each perfect word and letter may
> A seed of truth to you convey,
> As here the worthy Night of Pow'r
> Can germinate a waking ray.
>
> So with the turning world the hour,
> A ship at sea—unfurled the dow'r

Of strength in sail—by windbreath sped,
On time is borne. For thought to flow'r,

Within the sleeping dreamer's head
Prophetic aims to birth are bred,
A third of human time required
To incubate what will have led

The mind of day by impulse fired
At night, when mighty flame desired
To bear us on Buraq away
From petty care to life inspired.

The sight of strength, a means of peace,
For you can mean serene release
From fettered planning, as it meant
For One who nevermore would cease

To praise the angel that had sent
The spear to pierce the firmament,
The arrow-gold predicting morn
When, rapt, we'd hear the lesson lent.

Ev'n dreams of terror never scorn:
The medals that the brave adorn
Are gained in battle with the jinn
Who may the latter winner warn

Of weaknesses unknown within:
If we, repentant for our sin,
A warder-vigil will increase,
Far better that reward to win.

CONCLUDING THOUGHT: THE NAMING OF ANGELS

Wise Adam named the angels. This can we
Accomplish also. When Mnemosyne
And Zeus begot the Muses, didn't they
Create the waking flames of poetry?

The moments when we made our poems may
Be every one an angel named, to stay
Undying in the mind of him that penned,
Though resting till awakened on the day

When memory and maker effort lend
To resurrect what never had an end
But slept in earth of Eden to arise
On page of winter white, unaging friend.

The drive to write? A blest Buraq who flies
Where blue-illumined in the numen-skies
Prophetic angel of our memory,
World-self in vanished glory-spirit hies.

One hundred forty lyrics penned, unpent,
Surround me as I read, and bring the me's
Together that are gone: a glory gift
Must each be counted, re-encountered nigh,

Ev'n as the world, replete with objects new
In forms part-recognized, will overwhelm,
Delivered to a second life that came
In maker-breath, re-grant of Adam-skill.

My mission differs not: an angel sent
Was meant for latest naming-act that frees
A thunder heart and lightning glance—we sift
The wheat, yet no abandoned chaff will die

Without the potency to re-endue
The germing earth, her mind-enskying realm:
On my recital night, let angel-name
Be Morning Ray, the air with story fill.

SELECTED ANNOTATED BIBLIOGRAPHY

Abouleish, Ibrahim. *Sekem: A Sustainable Community in the Egyptian Desert.* Edinburgh: Floris, 2005. A biography of the community where I taught for a month, and of its founder. Central to the spiritual development of Dr. Abouleish have been his prayerful meditations on the ninety-nine names of Allah found in the Qur'an.

Alam, Shahid. *Gottespoesie: Kalligraphie Shahid Alam.* [no place or date of publication.].German translations of all the Qur'an passages are by Friedrich Rückert from the edition by Hartmut Bobzin.

———. *West-Ost-Begegnungen: Ausstellung zu Katharina Mommsens 85. Geburtstag.* Aachen, 1985. Photography, reproductions, and design by Horst Nogaisky. Illustrating its title, "West-East Encounters," the 20-page exhibition catalogue shows Alam as intercultural bridge builder, presenting calligraphies from works of Rilke, Goethe, Pakistani poet Ahmad Faraz, and others along with many Qur'an passages.

Ali, A. Yusuf, Translator. *The Holy Qur-an: Text, Translation, and Commentary.* McGregor & Werner, 1946. [First edition 1934.] Invaluable for its 6311 notes, plus appendices.

Bakhtin, Mikhail. *The Dialogic Imagination: Four Essays.* Michael Holquist, editor; Vadim Liapunov, editor and translator; Kenneth Brostrom, translator. Austin: University of Texas Press, 1982.

Bidney, Martin. *A Poetic Dialogue with Adam Mickiewicz: The "Crimean Sonnets" Translated, with Sonnet Preface, Sonnet Replies, and Notes.* Bonn: Bernstein-Verlag, 2007. The Polish poet combines Muslim and Catholic traditions in his imagery.

———. *East-West Poetry: A Western Poet Responds to Islamic Tradition in Sonnets, Hymns, and Songs.* Volume I in the Series: East-West Bridge Builders. Albany: State University of New York Press, 2010. My first book of Islam-related verse, 140 poems with an Introduction.

———. *Poems of Wine and Tavern Romance: A Dialogue with the Persian Poet Hafiz.* Volume III in the Series: East-West Bridge Builders. Albany: State University of New York Press, 2013. Contains 103 Hafiz poems with my verse replies.

Blake, William. *The Complete Poetry & Prose of William Blake.* Newly revised edition by Harold Bloom. Commentary by David Erdman. New York: Doubleday, 1988.

Bobzin, Hartmut, translator. *Der Koran: Neu übertragen von Hartmut Bobzin.* Verlag C.H. Beck [n.d.]. Scrupulously accurate, with 144 sura titles in calligraphies (plus all of Sura 1, "The Opening," as a calligraphic art work) by Shahid Alam.

Chittick, William C. *Divine Love: Islamic Literature and the Path to God*. Foreword by Seyyed Hossein Nasr. New Haven and London: Yale University Press, 2013. Perhaps the best introduction to Chittick's *oeuvre* of translation and research on spiritually inclusive thought and imagination in Islam.

Colpaert, Marc. *Where Two Seas Meet: Imagination, the Key to Intercultural Learning*. Translated by Ian Connerty and Guido Colpaert. Leuven, Belgium: Lannoo Campus Publishing House, 2009. See also on internet Colpaert's "Volledige [complete three-part] Interview met Martin Bidney over het project DIWANS," Platform Rond Mediawijsheid.

Eggers, Dave. *Zeitoun*. New York: Random, 2010.

Esposito, John L., Editor in Chief. *The Oxford Dictionary of Islam*. New York: Oxford, 2003.

——. *What Everyone Needs to Know about Islam*. New York: Oxford, 2011.

Feiler, Bruce. *Abraham: A Journey to the Heart of Three Faiths*. New York: HarperCollins, 2004. Affirmative but poignant, the book shows the Abraham story employed to engender unities, divisions.

——. *Where God Was Born: A Daring Adventure Through the Bible's Greatest Stories*. New York: HarperCollins, 2007.

FitzGerald, Edward, translator. *The Rubáiyát of Omar Khayyám*. First and fifth editions. Edited by Stanley Applebaum. New York: Dover, 1990.

Goethe, Johann Wolfgang von. *West-East Divan—The Poems with "Notes and Essays": Goethe's Intercultural Dialogues*. Translated, with Introduction and Commentary Poems, by Martin Bidney. "Notes and Essays" translation assisted by Peter Anton von Arnim. Volume II in the Series: East-West Bridge Builders. Albany: State University of New York Press, 2010. The introduction emphasizes Goethe's debt to medieval Persian pub poet Muhammad Shemseddin Hafiz, whom he called his "twin" (poem 26, "Unbounded" ["Unbegrenzt"]). Recitations based on several of my renderings were offered on BBC 3—Twenty Minutes, 2 episodes, "Goethe and the West-Eastern Divan," July 2012. These episodes were conceived in part as background for a BBC presentation of conductor Daniel Barenboim's West-East Divan Orchestra of Israelis and Palestinians.

Hafiz, Muhammad Shemseddin. *Der Divan von Mohammed Schemsed-din Hafis. Aus dem Persischen zum erstenmal übersetzt von Joseph von Hammer*. 2. vols. Stuttgart and Tübingen, 1812-1813 (1814). Repr. New York: Hildesheim, 1973. This is the "divan," or collection, which inspired that of Goethe in 1819.

Kris, Ernst. *Psychoanalytic Explorations in Art*. New York: Schocken, 1967.

Kuschel, Karl-Josef. *Juden Christen Muslime: Herkunft und Zukunft*. Düsseldorf: Patmos, 2007, 2nd edition 2008. Thoroughly grounded in close study of the three scriptures.

——. *Leben ist Brückenschlagen: Vordenker des interreligiösen Dialogs*. Düsseldorf: Patmos, 2011. Admirably wide-ranging, from Gandhi to Buber to Hans Küng.

Mommsen, Katharina. *Goethe und der Islam*. Frankfurt am Main: Insel Verlag, 2001.

———. *Goethe und die arabische Welt.* Frankfurt am Main: Insel Verlag. 1988. See my review in *Studies in Romanticism* 30:2 (1991), 294–98.

Pickthall, Marmaduke. *The Meaning of the Glorious Koran: An Explanatory Translation.* New York: Knopf, 1930. Repr. Everyman's Library, 1992. Poetically the finest version I have found in English.

Pushkin, Alexander. "*Kak Erivanskie Kovry*": *Zapadno-vostochnye Stikhi* / "*Like a Fine Rug of Erivan*": *West-East Poems* / "*Wie Teppiche aus Eriwan*": *West-östliche Gedichte,* "Voices of the World in Song" Vol. 2, Trilingual Edition with Introduction, illustrations, and audio book. Poems edited by Martin Bidney and Katharina Mommsen with "Introduction" by Bidney. Translated into English by Bidney from the Russian and recited in English by him. Published by the Mommsen Foundation. Free for downloading at martinbidney.com. Click any poem title to hear the lyric in Russian, English, or Michael Engelhard's German. A limited edition (300 copies) of this work is now in print (The Mommsen Foundation, Palo Alto / Global Scholarly Publications, New York, 2013). The "Introduction" (17) shows—evidently for the first time in Pushkin criticism—that the poet's lyric "The Prophet" ("Prorok") features a heart-excision strikingly akin to that of the Prophet Muhammad in a *hadith* cited by Annemarie Schimmel (see Schimmel 1985 below).

Rückert, Friedrich. *Schi-King: Chinesisches Liederbuch, gesammelt von Confucius, dem deutschen angeeignet von Friedrich Rückert.* Altona, bei I. J. Hammerich, 1833.

———. *Der Koran,* in Auszüge übersetzt von Friedrich Rückert. Hrsg. August Müller. Frankfurt/M, 1888. Though not complete, the best translation available in German.

Rüdiger, Horst, editor and compiler. *Griechische Gedichte mit Übertragungen deutscher Dichter.* Munich: Ernst Heimeran, 3rd edition 1936. Source of the Kallimachos ode I translate as part of the epigraph to poem 51.

Schimmel, Annemarie. *And Muhammad Is His Messenger: The Veneration of the Prophet in Islamic Piety.* Chapel Hill and London: University of North Carolina Press, 1985. See 67–69 for the *hadith* account of the "Opening of the Breast," which I show to be strikingly similar to Pushkin's "The Prophet" (see Pushkin above, "Introduction" xviii).

———. *My Soul Is a Woman: The Feminine in Islam.* Translated by Susan M. Ray. New York: Continuum, 2003.

———. *The Triumphal Sun: A Study of the Works of Jalāloddin Rumi.* Albany: State University of New York Press, 1993.

———, Editor. *Weltpoesie ist Weltversöhnung. Rückert zu Ehren eine Schriftenreihe der Friedrich Rückert Ges., 7).* Würzburg: Ergon, 1996.

Shah, Idries. *The Sufis.* "Introduction" by Robert Graves. New York: Doubleday, 1971.

Spinoza, Benedict [Baruch] de. *On the Improvement of the Understanding; the Ethics; Correspondence.* Translated by R. H. M. Elwes. New York: Dover, 1955.

INDEX

Aaron, 27
Abel, *xxxiv*, 117
Abouleish, Ibrahim, *vi, xlv*
Abraham, *xx, xxvii, xxx–xxxii, xli, xlv, xlvi*, 1, 18, 27, 32, 55, 70, 76, 89, 90, 112, 123, 164
   ethical teachings of, *xvii*
   in Qur'an, *xxx–xxxii*
   prayer of, 89, 90
Abraham: A Journey to the Heart of the Three Faiths (Feiler), *xxxi*
Abram (earlier name of Abraham), 18, 79
Abu Bakr, *xxxv*
Adam, *xxx, xxxv, xxxix–xl, xli*, 5, 6, 7, 10, 11, 14, 15, 27, 30, 45, 105, 169
Alam, Shahid, *vi, xiii, xvii, xxvi, xxvii, xliv, xlv*
Ali, A. Yusuf, *xxix, xxxix*, 71, 111, 139
"ALIF," Alam, Shahid, back cover, *xiii*
álif, xliv, 2, 5, 14, 156
Allah
   forgiveness by, *xxxvi, xxxvii, xl–xli*
   generosity of, *xxxvi, xxxvii–xxxix*
   metaphor use by, *xxxiv–xxxix*
   peace of mind granted by, *xxxvi, xxxix–xl*
   praise of, *xxii*, 1, 2, 3
   Qur'an of, *xvi–xx*, 4, 30, 32, 69, 111
   stewardship given by, *xli–xlii*
   Unifying Light of, *xxvi–xxvii*
"Allah-Menorah," *xiii, xxvii, xxviii*
allegory/allegoric, *xxviii*, 21, 24, 26, 99
alms/almsgiving, *xxxvii*, 20, 21, 41 (poor-due), 69, 141
androgyne/gynander, 114
angel(s), 59, 89, 123, 159, 165, 167, 169–170
anti-Mubarak revolution, *xxxiii*

Asiya (Pharaoh's wife), 95
AUM/OM, *xliv*, 33
Aziz (Islamic name corresponding to Potiphar), *xxxii, xxxiii*, 47, 50, 53

Babel, Tower of, *xxvii, xxxiv*, 43
Bakhtin, Mikhail, *xlv*
bard, *xxiv*, 49, 79
Baucis, *xxxiv*, 116
beautiful, *xv, xxxiv, xxxv, xxxviii, xliv, xlv*, 61, 72, 73, 140, 161
beauty, *vi, xv, xx, xxvi, xxxii, xxxvii–xxxviii*, 29, 35, 73, 111, 135
bee(s), 50, 51
Bible. *See* Hebraic/Hebrew Bible
bird(s), 30, 32, 35, 145
Bird in Flight (Brancusi), *xliii*
Blake, William, *xlv*
blind(ness), 32, 33, 153, 154, 160
Buddhist, *xxvi, xliv*, 46
Buraq, *xxxvi*, 23, 123, 167, 169

Cain, *xxiv*, 44, 117
candelabra, Sabbath, *xxvii*
cave, *xxxv*, 42, 134
centrality of metaphor, *xxiv–xxix*
chant, *xv, xxxviii*, 3, 4, 38, 130, 152, 165
Chapters of the Fathers (Talmudic tractate), 22
charity, *xxxvii*, 129, 141
Chittick, William C., *xliv*
Christian, *xv, xvi, xx–xxvi, xxvii, xxx–xxxi, xxxv, xxxix*, 9, 46, 82
Christian Gospels. *See* Gospels
Christianity, *xiii, xxvii, xxxv*, 1
chronotope, 22
Cimabue, 30
Colpaert, Marc, *xvi*

comfort, 114
compassion, *xxxi, xxxii, xxxiv, xl–xli*, 65, 80, 107
compulsion, none in religion, 15, 16–17

David, *xxxiv–xxxv, xli*, 27, 63, 76, 108, 116, 117
dawn, 26, 27, 166
Daybreak, *xvi*, 134
dead, brought forth, 36
deer, 34
deniers, 58
Deut. 6:4, Hear O Israel, *xx*
devil, 107, 142
dew, 3, 128, 134
Dhu 'n-Nun, 53
Dionysius the (pseudo-)Areopagite, *xxv*
Divan (Hafiz), *xliii*
divinity, *xl*, 111, 118
doubt, *xxvi*, 16, 24, 26, 55, 57, 62, 64, 130
dove, 18, 42, 115, 123, 134

earthly paradise, *xxviii–xxix*
ease, with hardship, 162, 163–165
East, *vi, xxiv*, 139
East-West Poetry (Bidney), *vii, xxxvi, xliv, xlvi*
Eber, 27
Ebusu'ud, *xl, xlv*, 126
Eden, *xxviii–xxix, xxxv, xxxix, xlii*, 7, 15, 44, 52, 71, 75, 79, 87, 105, 107, 125, 133, 138, 143, 145, 152, 155, 161, 164, 169. *See also* garden
Eggers, Dave, *xvi*
Egypt, *xxxiii*
Elijah, 27
Elisha, 27
emblem, *xiii, xx, xxv, xxvi, xxviii, xxix, xliv*, 2, 10, 11, 12, 57, 59, 62, 75, 85, 164
empathy, *xxxiv*, 10, 35, 57, 80, 91, 129
Enoch, 27
equanimity, *xxxix, xl*
Eser, Semih, *xlv*

Eve, *xxx, xl, xli*, 6, 7, 11
ewes, *xxxiv*, 117
Ezekiel, 27

"face" of the Lord, *xxvi*, 136
faith, *xxxvii, xxxviii, xlii*, 5, 12, 20, 44, 53, 55, 64, 65, 75, 77, 81, 95, 106, 148
faithful, *xli*, 12, 42, 45, 69, 87–88, 104, 141
fate, 18–19
Faust, 116
favor, *xxiv, xxxi, xxxiii, xxxv*, 17, 27, 57, 63, 72–75, 105, 115, 142, 153, 163
fear, 6
Feiler, Bruce, *xxxi, xxxii*
Finnegans Wake, xvi
fire, 13, 112
FitzGerald, Edward, *xliv*
fluid, gushing, 159
forgiveness, *xxxvi, xxxvii, xl–xli*, 20, 23, 52, 57, 102, 117, 122, 123, 133, 138
freedom, 74

Gabriel (Angel), *xvii, xx, xxv*, 12, 37, 40, 161, 165, 166
garden, *xxxviii, xli*, 4, 6, 20, 30, 44, 49, 64, 65, 74, 85, 89, 90, 95, 132, 138, 152. *See also* Eden
Garden of Abode, 138
generosity, *xxxvi, xxxvii–xxxix*
Gettysburg Address (Lincoln), *xxxvii*
Giotto, 30–31
Gnostic, 46
God, Sublime Similitude of, *xxv–xxvi*
Goethe, Johann Wolfgang von, *xxiv, xliii, xlv*, 126
Gospels, *xv, xvi, xvii, xxii, xxiv, xxxv*, 1, 9, 29, 30, 32, 40, 128
Gottespoesie, Alam, *xv, xxxviii*
grace, *xxxvii, xxxviii*, 1, 11, 12, 38, 40, 42, 63, 74, 75, 76, 79, 95, 107, 136, 142, 148, 153, 154, 157, 161, 163
grain, 18–19
gratitude, 43, 91

Griffith, Ralph T. H., *xxxiii*
guidance, *xvi*, 29
gyroscope, 77

Hafiz, Muhammad Shemseddin, *xliii, xliv,* 2, 126
Haman, *xxxiv*, 121
Hammer, Joseph von, *xliii, xlv*
"Hear O Israel," Judaism, *xx*
Heaven, 2, 42, 71, 77, 89, 150, 165
heaven(s), 1, 3, 8, 15, 20, 22, 23, 37, 68, 69, 72, 77, 86, 92, 95, 100, 102
heaven and earth, *xxv, xxix, xxxiv, xli,* 4, 5, 14, 24, 27, 32, 46–47, 53, 57, 59, 64–66, 79–80, 84, 96–97, 100, 102, 104–5, 109–10, 121, 123, 127, 136, 142, 166
Hebraic/Hebrew Bible, *xxii, xxv*
Hebrew, *xxxiii, xxxiv, xli,* 63, 95, 121
Hegel, G.W.F., *xliv*
hell, 55, 109
Hindu, *xliv*
hoarding, *xxxvii, xxxix,* 70, 86, 142, 143, 162
Homer, *xlv*
Horace, *xlv*
hour, 103
Houri, 87
hymn, *xli, xlii,* 1, 5, 45, 57, 63, 76, 90, 93, 101, 102, 103, 123, 147, 150, 152, 158

Iblis, 39, 105, 117. *See also* Satan
illumination/illumine, *xvi, xix, xxii–xxiii, xxv, xxvii, xxxvi, xliv,* 1, 49, 61, 77, 138, 169
"ILM," cover, *xiii, xxvi*
Iqbal, Muhammad, 18
"IQRA" ("Recite!"), *xiii, xx, xxi*
Isaac, 27, 70
Isaiah, 63
Ishmael, 27
Islam, holy books of, *xvi*
Islamic Qur'an, *xv*
Islamic tradition, influences from, *xliii–xlvi*

Jacob, *xxxii,* 27, 37, 51, 52, 53, 65, 70, 158
Jami, *xxxiii*
Jeremiah, 63
Jesus, *xvii, xxx, xxxi, xxxix, xxxv,* 1, 27, 29–32, 68–69, 75–76, 123
  Qur'an parable of, *xlv*
  Spirit of God, *xvii*
Jethro, 27
Jew, 46
Jewish, *xvi, xx, xxii–xxiv, xxvii, xxx, xxxv*
jinn(s), *xxiv,* 16, 59, 104, 105, 148, 167
Job, *xxxv,* 27, 39, 76
John, *xvi*
John the Baptist, *xxx, xxxv,* 27, 75, 76
Jonah, *xvii, xxxv, xlvi,* 15, 27, 43, 44, 45, 46, 76, 114, 115
Joseph, *xvii, xxx, xliii,* 27, 37, 39, 47, 51–53
  in Qur'an, *xxxii–xxiv*
journey(ing), 22, 85, 155
Joyce, James, *xvi*
Judaism, *xxvii*
  "Hear O Israel," *xx*
Juden Christen Muslime (Kuschel), *xxxi*
judgment, *xxii,* 1, 2, 3, 43, 46, 76
jugular, 130
Jujube Tree, 138

Kaaba, 92
kaleidoscope, 77
Kallimachos, 61
Keats, John, *xxx*
Khayyám, Omar, *xliv*
kindness, *xxxi, xxiv, xxxv, xli,* 6, 9, 80, 82, 105
King of Kings, 38, 122
Kris, Ernst, 30
Koran, *xvi, xvii, xxxviii. See also* Qur'an
Kuschel, Karl-Josef, *xxxi–xxxii*

Laila, 79
lamp, 24
Leben ist Brückenschlagen (Kuschel), *xxxi*
lenitude, 6

Leonardo da Vinci, 131
leper, 32
light, 25, 36, 41, 84, 127, 160
likeness, *xxxviii, xliii,* 18, 20, 24, 29, 30, 32, 65, 66, 89, 96, 97, 128, 137, 150, 155
   uniting theme of, *xxiv–xxix*
Lincoln, Abraham, *xxxvii*
litigants, *xxxix,* 117
loan(s), 142
"Lord of the Daybreak," *xvi, xxvii.* See also Daybreak
   Qur'an of Allah, *xvi–xx*
Lot, 27, 76
love, as unifying moral light, *xxxvi–xlii*
lower soul, 49
Luke, *xxxv, xlv,* 82

Mark, *xvi*
Mary, *xvii, xxx, xxxv,* 30, 32, 68–72, 75, 164
Matthew, *xvi, xlv*
Matt. 6:9, Our Father, *xxii*
Mecca, *xxxiv, xxxvii,* 12, 77, 123
meditation, *xvi, xxvi, xliv,* 62, 74, 89, 155
Mehmet II, *xlv,* 12
mercy, *xxx, xxxi, xxxiii, xl–xlii,* 1, 3, 7, 14, 22, 23, 36, 37, 39, 40, 49, 53, 55, 56, 70, 76, 86, 87, 90, 93, 95, 96, 107, 123
messenger(s), 85, 93
Messiah, 66, 69
metaphor, *xv, xxiv, xxx, xliii,* 10, 11, 24, 28, 29, 38, 41, 64, 65, 66, 77, 97, 136, 139, 150, 158, 166
   bird, 30, 32, 145
   cave, *xxxv,* 42, 134
   centrality of, *xxiv–xxix*
   dove, 18, 42, 115, 123, 134
   garden, *xxxviii, xli,* 4, 6, 20, 30, 44, 49, 64, 65, 74, 85, 89, 90, 95, 132, 138, 152
   grain, 18–19
   lamp, 24
   mountain crashing, *xxvii,* 38
   rock, *xxviii,* 10, 20, 111

vat, 11
well, *xlii,* 12, 108, 158
Mickiewicz, Adam, *xxiv*
mindfulness, *xliv,* 14
mode of action, love, *xxxvi–xlii*
Mommsen, Katharina, *vi, xlv,* 35, 145
"Morning Hours, The," Sura 93 of Qur'an, qtd., *xxxvii*
   in Rücket's version, *xxxviii*
Morning Star, *xxvii,* 157
Moses, *xvii, xxvii, xxxiv,* 10, 27, 38, 39, 70, 73, 93, 95, 121, 123, 158
Muhammad, 1, 4, 9, 15, 26, 27, 29, 32, 33, 38, 39, 42, 45, 57, 64, 65, 68, 69, 70, 72, 74, 93, 110, 123, 126, 128, 134, 137, 146, 147, 148, 161
   Prophet in Qur'an, *xvii–xviii*
   and Qur'an, *xxvii, xxxv–xxxvi*
"Muhammad's Calling," Rilke, *xviii–xx*
"Musa, Issa, Muhammad" ("Moses, Jesus, Muhammad"), *xiii, xix*
Muses, 169
Muslims, presence in world, *xvii*
mystical, 73

Naboth, *xxxiv,* 116
names, of God, *vi, xv,* 65, 72, 73, 89, 140, 150
narratives, parable, *xxix–xxxvi*
Night of Power, Qur'an, *xxv,* 140, 166. See also Recital Night
Noah, *xvii, xxxi,* 27, 76, 123
"Nurullah, Ruhullah, Habibullah" ("Light of God, Spirit of God, Love of God"), *xiii, xviii*

omens, 35
"Opening, The," Sura 1 of Qur'an, *xxii, xxiv*
Ophite Gnostic, 46
orphan, 161
"Our Father," Christianity, *xx, xxii*

parable, *xxiv–xxvi, xxix, xxx, xxxiv–xxxv,* 8, 38, 41, 66, 116, 118, 154
   of Jesus, *xlv*
   narratives of scriptural people, *xxix–xxxvi*
parabola, 56, 118
pardon, *xxxi, xxxii, xl–xli,* 22, 23, 39, 49, 52, 71, 74, 89, 90, 107, 123, 126, 133, 138. *See also* forgiveness
peace, *xxix,* 60, 167
peace of mind, *xxxvi, xxxix–xl*
pen(s), 100, 159
Pentateuch, *xvi, xxv*
Pharaoh, *xvii, xxxiv,* 95, 121
Philemon, *xxxiv,* 116
Pickthall, Mohammed Marmaduke, *xv, xlvi,* 157
Plato, *xxvi*
poet, *xxiii–xxvii, xxix, xxxi, xl, xliv,* 11, 24, 30, 36, 38, 49, 53, 61, 63, 89, 90, 96, 97, 135, 137, 159, 166
poetry, *xv, xxiii–xxiv, xxxiv, xlii, xliv,* 10, 118, 158, 169
poor, 21
poor-due (alms), 40
Potiphar (Hebrew scripture name corresponding to Islamic Aziz), *xxxii*
Potiphar's wife, *xxxii,* 47, 51, 53. *See also* Zulaikha, Zuleika
pride, 5. *See also* tyrant
prophet(s), *xvii, xxiv, xxv, xxxi,* 70, 113, 134
   of Islam, 27
   Prophet, *xx, xxiv, xxvii, xxix, xxxiii, xxxv, xl, xliii,* 18, 22, 26, 27, 29, 40, 39, 61, 63, 66, 69, 75, 95, 97, 102, 107, 110, 123, 137, 146, 149, 150, 161, 165, 166. *See also* Muhammad
   in Qur'an, *xxvi–xxvii, xxix, xxxv, xl, xliv,* 9
prostration (in prayer), 101, 159
prudence, *xli*
Psalms, *xvi, xxxv,* 63

purity, 133
Pushkin, Alexander, *xxiv*

qiblah, 12
Queen of Sheba, *xvii, xliii,* 44, 92
Qur'an, *xxiv,* 9, 18, 30, 38, 39, 41, 45, 49, 57, 64–66, 71, 74, 77, 87, 96, 111, 118, 128, 136, 137, 139, 141, 148, 156. *See also* Koran
   Abraham in, *xxx–xxxii*
   of Allah, *xvi–xx,* 4, 30, 32, 69, 111
   chanting or hearing of, *xv*
   Mary, Jesus, and John the Baptist in, *xxxv*
   Moses, David, and Solomon in, *xxxiv*
   Muhammad's life in, *xxxv–xxxvi*
   Night of Power in, *xxv. See also* Recital Night
   Prophet Muhammad in, *xvii–xviii*
   structure of, *xv*

Rabi'a, *xliii,* 92
Ramadan, *xxxvii*
reassurance, 42, 101
Recital Night, 62, 123, 144. *See also* Night of Power
recompense, 119
remembrancer, *xlvi,* 57, 68
responsibility, *xli*
responsive, 124, 143
resurrection, 37
rhythm, *xv, xix, xxxii, xxxvii, xxxviii, xlv,* 30
Rilke, Rainer Maria, *xviii–xx*
rivers, 10
rock, 10, 20, 111
rosa mundi (flower), 35
Rückert, Friedrich, *xxiii, xxxviii*
Rumi, Mevlana, *xliii,* 77

Sabaean, 9
Sáleh, 27

Salsabil, 150
Satan, *xxxvi*, 6, 7. *See also* Iblis
satori, *xliv*, 37
Schimmel, Annemarie, *xliii–xliv*, 53, 92, 161
sciencecrypture, 13
scope, 22–23
scripture, *xx, xxii, xxiv–xxv, xxxiii, xxxvii*, 1, 53, 68, 69, 70, 72, 79, 85, 122
    of Allah, 4, 30, 32, 69, 111
    Gospel/Christian, *xvi, xvii, xxii, xxiv, xxxv*, 1, 9, 29, 30, 32, 40, 128
    Hebraic/Hebrew Bible, *xxi, xxvi*
    parable narratives of scriptural people, *xxix–xxxvi*
    Qur'an, *xv, xvii, xx, xxiv, xxix, xxxv, xxxvi*, 26, 29
    Torah/Jewish, *xvi, xxiv, xxx*, 1, 9, 30, 32, 40, 63, 128
sculptor, Christ as, 30
sea(s), 100
seer, 51, 72, 103, 134, 145
Serene Joy of Shared Wonder, Three Texts, One Light, *xx, xxii–xxiv*
serenity, *xxxix*, 69
service, 80
Seth, 44
Shah, Idries, *xliv*
Sheba. *See* Queen of Sheba
similitudes, *xxxiv–xxix*, 8, 17, 24, 38, 64–67, 84, 85, 96, 97–98, 118, 122, 127, 137, 147, 166
singer, *xlvi*, 3, 45, 97, 134
slander, 129
Solomon, *xxx, xxxiv–xxxv, xlii–xliii*, 27, 76, 92, 104, 105, 108
song, 3, 86, 91, 125
spend wealth, 21, 141, 142
spider, 42
Spinoza, Baruch, *xlv*, 82
spirit, *xxii, xxiv, xxvii, xxix, xxxviii, xl, xliv*, 15–16, 20, 22, 33, 52, 57, 62, 71, 75–76, 80, 84, 90–93, 97, 102–4, 108, 110, 117–18, 126–27, 129–30, 149, 156–58, 160, 162 169
    fiery, *xviii, xx, xxxiv*
    wing, 22, 103
Spirit of God, *xvii, xxx, xxxv*, 13, 31, 32, 45, 81, 120, 146–48, 156, 166
stairway(s), 146, 147
state of being, love, *xxxvi–xliii*
stewardship, *xxxvi–xxxvii, xli–xlii*, 11, 107
stork(s), *xlv*, 99
Sublime Similitude, *xxv, xxvi, xxix*, 66–67, 96, 97–98
Sufi wisdom, *xliv*, 91, 120, 137, 138
The Sufis (Idries Shah), *xliv*
Suleika, 53. *See also* Zulaikha, Zuleika
Sun, 160
Superluminous Darkness, *xxv*
surrender, *xxix*, 27–28
suspicion, 129
symbol, *xxiv–xxv, xxvi, xxvii, xxx, xxxiii–xxxv*, 2, 10, 11, 12, 53, 66–67, 109, 111, 122
symbols' symbol (God), 38

Taj Mahal, *xxvi*
Talmud 2:21, 22
Tarfon, Rabbi, 22
tear(s), 5, 134
Three Texts, One Light: Serene Joy of Shared Wonder, *xx, xxii–xxiv*
titans, 5. *See also* pride
Torah, *xvi, xxiv*, 1, 9, 29, 30, 32, 40, 63, 128
Tower of Babel, *xxvii, xxxiv*
tower (of Pharaoh), 121
tranquillity, *xxxix, xl*, 38, 42, 44, 71, 78, 149
travel, 21
Tree of Life, 11, 107
trust, *xli–xliii*, 5, 49, 54, 104, 105, 107. *See also* stewardship
tyrant, *xli–xlii*, 5, 15, 104, 105, 107, 116, 121. *See also* pride

unifying light, *vi, xv*
unlettered, Muhammad as, 26

vat, 11
veil(s), 24, 33, 54
vigil, 149, 167
vision, *xxvi, xxxii, xxxv,* 52, 89, 111, 113, 160

water, 26, 36, 86
wave, 138
well, *xlii*, 12, 108, 158
West, *vi, xxxiv,* 139
West-East Divan (Goethe), *xlv*
Where God Was Born (Feiler), *xxxi*
witness, Muhammad as, 102

worm, *xxxiv,* 108–109

Yokheved (Moses' mother), 95
Yusuf and Zulaikha: A Poem by Jami (Griffith), *xxxiii*

Zachariah, 27, 75, 76
Zanjabil, 150
zarra (particle), 138
Zeitoun (Eggers), *xvi*
Zeitoun, Abdulrahman, *xvi*
Zeus, 169
Zoroastrian, 46
Zulaikha, *xxxii, xxxiii,* 53
Zuleika, *xxii, xxxiii, xxxii,* 47, 49, 50, 53